DETOUR

DETOUR

LOSE YOUR WAY – FIND YOUR PATH

S. Mariah Rose

atmosphere press

dedicated
to spiritual seekers everywhere.
may you find what you're looking for where you least
expect it...

CONTENTS

TURNING IN THE RIGHT DIRECTION

Directions are instructions given to explain how. Direction is a vision offered to explain why.

~ Simon Sinek

When I visited Santa Fe for the first time in the spring of 1988 at the age of twenty-eight, my loneliness was so complete that I felt almost invisible.

I had come to Santa Fe from my home in Boulder, Colorado, to visit Nellie. Nellie was my spiritual teacher of sorts. But mainly she was my friend—my eccentric friend. Nellie had an awareness of things just beyond form—of things intangible but somehow real, more real than everyday life. Nellie would know what to tell me about the mess my life was in, I thought.

I was married, but not happily so. I was a college graduate but chronically under-employed. I had a lot of friends, but I felt isolated.

I had met Nellie when I first came out west, so I had known her nearly ten years. She had been introduced to me by mutual friends and instantly became a surrogate mother figure, as she was twenty years my senior.

Nellie lived with her three young children in a ramshackle farmhouse outside Boulder. She was a practitioner of Jin shin jitsu, an ancient Japanese form of energy healing, similar to Reiki. She was the quintessential hippie mom; she wore flowing skirts, baked her own bread, and raised goats and chickens that were perpetually running about her yard.

With her kids in and out of the place all the time, her home was pure organized chaos like I had never seen before. It was a joy and a relief to me to know someone so kind and disorganized and giving all at the same time. It was a stark contrast to my childhood back east, which was suburban, orderly, and sterile.

What I loved most about Nellie was her no-nonsense attitude. She was brash, bold, independent, and nobody was going to push her around. She lived simply but happily, and she lived life on her own terms.

When she had left Boulder for Santa Fe several years previous, we had remained friends from a distance. I had remained in Boulder, living with my husband Michael while working as a massage therapist and freelance magazine writer.

When Michael and I began having problems, it was Nellie who I called, not my own mother.

One evening in March, I phoned her after Michael and I had one of our circular conversations about our future that went nowhere and left both of us spent and exhausted. He had left, angry. I did not know when, or if, he would be back. In truth, a part of me didn't care, so tired was I of the stuck energy around our relationship.

"I just don't know what to do," I said. I tried not to cry on the phone to her, but I'm sure she could hear my voice quiver.

"Sara, you should really come and see me here in New Mexico," Nellie said.

"Sure, why not?" I said.

"And seriously consider coming here to live. The land is peaceful and beautiful. There is so much open space."

I can't leave Michael, I thought. I'm ready to settle down. I want to have a family someday. How does moving to Santa Fe fit into these plans, I wondered.

"And I have moved into an adobe home, it's really amazing. You'd like it," added Nellie.

"Then I've got to get Michael to agree to come with me. Maybe it'll be just what we need to get ourselves out of the rut we're in," I said.

Nellie said nothing. She was not a big fan of marriage, having been married and divorced twice with three kids total and not a penny of child support to show for it. But, she always got by.

Because I was feeling so lost and hopeless and because I trusted Nellie so completely, I made concrete plans to visit her in Santa Fe right then and there; and to realistically assess the feasibility of moving there.

I approached my upcoming visit with a sense of urgency. More importantly than moving or not moving to Santa Fe, I had to figure out if my marriage to Michael was actually something that would work. If not, I had to end it and then figure out what to do next.

I left for Santa Fe a week or so after speaking to Nellie. I barely remember the drive from Boulder, so preoccupied was I with thoughts of doom and gloom about my life. The stakes were high for this visit. I had to make a move one way or the other; both physically, to settle down somewhere and create some stability for my life and mentally, to move out from under this dark place I was in. I craved a more joyful outlook on life.

I felt like I was slowly coming unraveled. Everything I

had known to be true about my life and the direction it should be taking was in flux. I was about to come to face-to-face with a deep void and the harder I tried to avoid it, the closer it loomed.

I felt like I was clinging to a raft that was headed for rapids and the only thing I could do was to hold on for dear life and brace myself for the bumpy ride that was imminent. There was no controlling the outcome, and I knew it. And it was really scary.

I had been raised to believe in the illusion of control. If I did what was "right," my life would be predictable, follow certain familiar themes, I would turn out to be "successful." I had deviated course unintentionally and now I was left believing that something terrible was going to happen to me. But what, exactly, I did not know.

I pulled up in front of Nellie's adobe house at dusk. She came out to greet me with a big smile and a bear hug. Despite her sun-creased face and wispy salt and pepper hair that had come partially undone from its ponytail in back and now blew every which way, Nellie was still pretty. She was in her late 40s. Her kids, a boy and two girls, ran around the yard and came shyly over to me as they saw Nellie and I embrace.

Aaron, the oldest, grabbed my little suitcase.

"Put it in Kate's room," Nellie instructed him. Sara can sleep in there tonight."

"Mom," Kate protested. "Where will I sleep?"

"Shush, we talked about it already. You can share a room with your sister while we have company. Now show Sara some respect."

"I like it when Sara visits," Willow, the middle child, said in a small happy voice.

All of Nellie's kids were blond, blue-eyed, and tan. They spent all their free time playing outside, running around freely in the fresh air.

I loved being with Nellie and her kids. It was a vicarious way for me to re-live my own childhood and watching Aaron, Willow, and Kate laugh, shout and feel at ease in nature and with their vivid childish emotions gave me a pang of agony in my side as I remembered my own childhood, which was vastly different.

Growing up in New England, my parents were university professors in a small town. The feeling that everyone was watching me was constraining. I dared not make a mistake and when I inevitably did as a teenager, drinking and wrecking a car, everyone knew and judged me—not just my parents but also the whole town. At least it had seemed that way.

I was a latchkey kid, coming home from school alone to an empty house in the suburbs of Kingston, Rhode Island, a college town. I didn't go out for track or cheerleading or even join the drama club. Even in those days, I wasn't a joiner.

Life in the suburbs, coveted and desired by my parents, was for me merely a jungle of emptiness and boredom, which festered and led to restlessness for something unseen.

Being in Santa Fe with Nellie and her kids was about as far away as I could get from there—that time—that place—those feelings.

I looked around at Nellie's simple but comfortable adobe home. A fluffy couch was draped with several Mexican blankets. Plants of various sizes crowded every window. Nellie had a green thumb. I sat at a round oak table, kids' books, crumbs, a child's unfinished drawing, and a toy mouse meant for a cat, hand-woven placemats in front of me.

Behind me in Nellie's narrow kitchen dirty dishes remained in the sink. At that moment, she disappeared, and I just sat there. I could see a plaque hanging above her gas stove that read, "Whatever works elsewhere, doesn't work in Santa Fe," written on it in fancy cursive letters.

What the hell is that supposed to mean, I wondered.

After getting settled into Kate's room, Nellie and I spent hours talking at her kitchen table, with a cat curled up on my lap, another sleeping on top of the table next to my plate: piping hot homemade tortilla dripping with honey, a mug of herbal tea in hand.

"Sara, have you ever considered going on a vision quest?" Nellie asked me.

"A what?" I asked.

"I want you to go into the mountains alone and fast and ask for a vision," Nellie instructed me in a matter-of-fact tone. "I volunteer to provide you transportation to and from a destination that I think would be perfect," she added.

I had never gone into the mountains alone or even conceived of asking for a vision. But Nellie was not someone to argue with. I didn't say anything.

"In many Native American traditions both men and women were expected to go on vision quests in early adulthood," Nellie said. I recognized her facial expression; she looked like she had a secret she was letting me in on.

"It was considered a vital rite of passage that I think should be revisited in this day and age."

"I don't know," I said, taking a sip of my peppermint

tea and blotting my lips with my napkin. "I feel pretty scared just thinking about it."

Then Nellie pulled one of her classic moves. "Sara," she nearly screamed, slapping the table. "Why do you think I invited you down here? To sunbathe, shop, and hang out with my kids and my cats?"

Yes, I thought. Why in the world not?

Nellie continued. "My guides told me it was time for something more meaningful."

I had gotten used to the way Nellie spoke over the years. Once in a while she would mention her "guides," which I interpreted to be spiritual urgings or internal voices that seemed to provide her with paranormal wisdom.

"Then I guess I'll go," I said uneasily, feeling instantly glad that I had thrown my little orange and red two-man tent from Sears into the trunk of my car before I left. When dealing with Nellie, one could never be too prepared. I knew this from previous adventures with her, planned and unplanned.

I sensed seriousness in Nellie's tone, and I knew that I really had to do something. I was uncomfortable with the sense that I was drifting in my life, having been raised to be goal-oriented. I needed to come up with a "what's next" plan that made sense and felt right.

"Good!" Nellie straightened. She whisked away a fly that had been feasting on a droplet of honey on the table.

"I'm going to bed," she announced, with a huge grin. "I'll see you bright and early in the morning."

I was beginning to wish I hadn't come. I wanted to be with Michael all of a sudden. Just the feel of his arms around me would help me to forget that things had gone so terribly wrong between us, even if just for a moment. I wanted that now.

I went to bed alone.

I did not sleep well that night. I tossed and turned in the tiny bed that belonged to Nellie's youngest daughter, who was no more than six. The bed was too small, the room unfamiliar. The air outside was still and made my incessant thoughts seem all the more raucous.

I kept thinking of Michael. Michael and I had met in New York four years earlier, I had been living in Manhattan going to college at the New School and supporting myself as a massage therapist at a women's health club.

I was 24 years old and hadn't been seriously involved with anyone for a couple of years. I watched as former high school friends were embarking on careers, getting married, buying homes, and starting families.

I had felt like life was passing me by.

When I first laid eyes on Michael it was at a reggae club in New York. Across the body-strewn, fluorescent-lit, open room, pulsating with deafening reggae music, I felt woozy.

What a great dancer! I thought. Michael was tall and lanky; his sandy hair was tousled, and his hazel eyes flirted with me from a distance.

I meandered across the dance floor to where he was gyrating and began swaying nearby. When our eyes connected, I thought I'd reached nirvana. His smile was glorious; he brushed my arm with subtle confidence and motioned me onto the dance floor in front of him. We began to dance wildly together oblivious of our surroundings, drinking and kissing intensely as the night turned into an exhausted dawn.

I knew I had to have Michael. I wanted to possess him. I became obsessed with him as our romance ensued. From the start, it was tangled with confused desire and mixed messages.

Michael was Belgian. He had arrived in New York at twenty-two from a little village with big dreams and nothing but his good looks to fall back on. And then his luck changed for the better: he met me.

I sighed audibly in the darkness and wiped away a tear.

Although I loved Michael with my entire being, I was starting to feel that he had simply used me to stay in America. Our marriage was hastily arranged. Our families were kept out of the decision, at least until we were legally paired. It was good at first, but for the past year, it hadn't been.

Still, I wasn't ready to call it quits just yet... my thoughts were relentless and repetitive, going nowhere, giving me no peace.

Miraculously the morning came. Although according to Nellie's directive, I would be fasting throughout the evening and night, she took pity on me and served me breakfast: homemade pancakes and fresh melon. In spite of the fact that the kids were energetic and playful, my mood had turned somber. I barely acknowledged them as I ate in silence and, as anticipated, began to prepare for my vision quest.

I packed a bag of apples to eat, along with my little tent, a warm sleeping bag, several more gallons of water, and warm clothes in my backpack. I knew to dress in layers to ward off the cold of the high-altitude desert at night. Nellie lent me her down jacket, just in case it got really, really cold she said. A down jacket was something I actually didn't think to bring, having no idea that I would be cast out into the wilderness at night, alone, cold and hungry by my dear friend.

"Sara," Nellie said, interrupting my morose inner dialogue, "You will be fine, I know it. Just remain calm and ask to be shown what your next steps are to be."

"I know," I whined, "But this doesn't seem like it'll be much fun."

"Fun is overrated," Nellie reasoned.

"You're right." I sighed.

I felt myself come to grips with the certainty that I was truly going on a vision quest and that I would be alone for the night in the wilderness.

"Let's go," I said to Nellie. "Ready or not, here I come."

Nellie drove me out of town later that morning, far into the purple hills. As we drove, I inhaled deeply and smelled dust and sage.

To contemplate being alone like this was terrifying, yet it thrilled me. I knew it was something I had to do. I was unused to silence, open spaces in nature, and extended periods of time spent in the depths of my own thoughts. I didn't talk much as we left town.

I could sense Nellie giving me sideways glances periodically as she maintained her focus on the road. I knew my being quiet was okay. I never had to pretend with Nellie, so I just relaxed as my thoughts drifted back to my childhood.

I don't remember a childhood filled with lazy sunny afternoons, watching the clouds float by like cotton candy. Instead, it was a strife-filled time. I remember a lot of screaming: Screaming and chaos and emotional scenes that didn't make sense. There was a sense of urgency about things, most of the time, both at home and in the world at large.

By the time I left home and headed west to Boulder on my own at age eighteen, I had my escape mechanisms firmly in place. I would ride any freight train that pulled into the station, whether it be a man, a drug, a drink, or new adventure, I was on board for whatever I could get, and then some.

The impact of my childhood upon my life's choices stretched onward, far into my early adulthood as I struggled to grapple with an inner pain that seemed to have no end. Even now, almost thirty, married, a college degree, on my own for more than ten years already, I still felt that hollowness that I was beginning to realize could not be filled by anything in the outside world. It felt like I needed something more within.

It was for this reason that I had decided to follow Nellie's suggestion, push through my fear, and spend the night alone in the desert.

"How're you doin'?" Nellie finally ventured, breaking the silence as we approached our destination.

"Ugh, I don't know," I said. "My stomach hurts and my palms are sweaty."

"You'll be safe here I promise," she said reassuringly. "I'll pick you up at noon tomorrow, about twenty-four hours from now."

While I sensed Nellie was ready to leave, needing to get back to her world of children and Jin shin jitsu sessions, she got out of the van with me and helped me unload my gear.

It was going to be a long twenty-four hours.

In spite of my genuine apprehension, I looked around

at my surroundings. I felt awed by the stark beauty that surrounded me. Pinion and sage-covered dry hillsides, deep green and massive; jagged gray cliffs off in the distance.

"Are you okay?" Nellie asked me with a deep penetrating look.

"Yeah," I sighed.

"Okay, I really mean this, Sara—have fun!" she said as she turned to go, winking at me with her head craned around as she was walking away. Then she came back and hugged me good and strong.

"Good bye and good luck," she said with her trademark wide grin.

I hugged her back and then watched as she walked to her van, got in and drove out of the National Forest parking lot, her van bouncing down the road in swirls of red dust.

I heard a coyote howl in the distance and a shiver went up my spine. Somewhat mechanically I pitched my tiny orange Sears tent in a clearing by a little stream. I stashed my supplies of water and apples inside, along with my sleeping bag and backpack filled with layers of warm and cool clothes: shorts and a tee-shirt, thermal socks, sweat pants, several polar fleece shirts and Nellie's down jacket, just in case.

I tried not to think too much about anything as I worked. Just focus on the tasks at hand, I told myself. When I was finished, I set off on a short hike with the inner caution to not stray too far from my "home," the small clearing beside the softly running stream that was my tent site.

I followed a trail beside the stream that climbed a bit

and as I walked, I felt my breath catch in my throat. I felt proud that I had come, exhilarated by the possibilities that opened up to me as I discovered my ability to go outside my comfort zone and do something outrageous and courageous at the same time: spend a night alone in the wilderness.

The trail took me up a hill where the stream lay below me. Across from me was a sheer gray and black rock wall. Because of the angle of the sun at my back, I could see my shadow perfectly against the rock face on the other side of the stream from where I stood.

I waved at myself, and my shadow-self waved back. The shadow's long hair fluttered in the breeze as I felt my own hair being lifted up and tousled around my head. I imagined that my shadow self was actually my "double," something I remember reading about in one of Carlos Castaneda's books.

She was the brave me, the wise me, the all-knowing spiritual part of me who would guide the human me, as long as I remembered to ask her for direction and to listen to her answer. I wonder if that's really true, I asked myself. Is there a part of me that is All-Knowing?

No, I was playing a mind game with myself, as I tried to occupy myself in the silence and to keep myself from getting fearful or from trying too hard to figure anything out. I knew if I struggled for an answer none would come. And if I relaxed and stopped thinking about a problem over and over, an answer would appear suddenly when I was least expecting it.

I must have gotten lost in my thoughts and the peacefulness of my surroundings because before long, the sun began to go down. Nellie told me these sunsets that seem to last for an eternity in the Southwest were termed an "afterglow." Although it should have been completely dark, the reflection of the deep orange sun lingered over the horizon, illuminating the earth in an unnatural brightness.

Suddenly, it was a brilliant star-studded evening. As I stood there looking around, I had a feeling of well-being come over me that was unexpected and unexplained. I was alone in the desert at night for the first time in my life, adrift in my priorities, uncertain just about everything that had to do with my future and yet I felt at peace. It was a small miracle.

The peace came from the landscape, and, more importantly, from the silence. No cars, TV, phone, people talking, list of "to dos." I took a deep breath, smiled inwardly.

I ate an apple for dinner and drank some water, which tasted wonderful. The hike had made me thirsty. My stomach growled. I was hungry. I shivered, this time from genuine cold. I put Nellie's down jacket on over my clothes and climbed into my sleeping bag.

In spite of being exhausted and starving, I knew that this was it. I had to ask for a vision and to hope that it came. What if nothing happened, I thought. What if I lay here all night and did not sleep a wink and no vision appeared. I need to calm down, I thought.

I heard more coyotes howling and tried to reassure myself that they were far off in the distance. Eventually, after what seemed like hours but was probably only minutes, I began to warm up in my sleeping bag and succeeded in willing myself to relax.

As I was drifting off to sleep in my little tent to the

sweet sound of gently flowing water, I remembered to ask for a vision. I fell into a sound sleep.

Sometime during the night, I found myself awake. Then, without any fanfare, and as if it were the most ordinary event in the world, my vision came. It seemed so matter of fact that I wasn't even that excited. Probably because I told myself I was making it up rather than really experiencing it. But I let it happen nonetheless, enjoying the dreamlike quality of the vision as it revealed itself.

A circle of men, women, and children holding hands was spread out over a huge grassy meadow at the base of a mesa. It was another time, maybe 200 years ago and everyone was dressed in buckskins and blankets, feathers in their hair and moccasins on their feet. A chorus of drummers pounded out a steady rhythm in the background and several warriors on horseback traversed the tribal circle.

I was seated in the center of the meadow, inside the warmth of the group and outside, looking at the scene from above, at the same time. I was there and not there; I was a part of and apart from. But the sensations running through my veins were undeniable.

Sacred ground—home. The gently flowing river, the soothing pines, which radiated a subtle fresh scent, the full moon glowing, illuminating the rolling dusty hills, all were peaceful, comforting, enveloping me in the land, calling me back to some unknown roots in space and time, indenting upon my sensory and visual memory the image and sensation of belonging.

The sky became my father; wise and all-knowing. I felt a completeness I had never known. And all was perfect and blessed and eternal. I fell asleep, rocked like a baby in the arms of a tender caregiver.

A cool breeze shook the pines slightly. The stream gurgled and the earth opened up its arms and cradled me becoming my mother, nurturing and all-forgiving.

Without understanding the vision, I intuitively knew what it meant: my next step was to move to Santa Fe, New Mexico, to live. The simplicity and ease with which this knowledge washed over me was astonishing. Yet it felt solid, real, and workable.

I had been given an answer to my question. I was relieved. Things made sense to me then for a brief moment in the middle of the night. The connection that the Native Americans had to the land and their ability to live in harmony with nature was what stood out for me about this vision. I was left with the impression somehow that the land on which I was lying in the middle of the night was, for me, a safe haven where I could live peacefully and where I was, in essence, being guided toward.

The next morning, however, was far from tranquil. In fact, it was jarring. I awoke freezing and hungry. Eating a chilled apple and drinking icy water from my water bottle didn't warm my body or my mood. Doubt had crept in and greeted me with a scowl. As I peered out of my tent, I felt swallowed up by the enormity of the landscape surrounding me that, the night before, had seemed so gentle and comforting.

I noticed the sun was peeking above the highest rock crest. I looked at my watch. 7:15 a.m.

Five more hours and I'm outta here.

My decision to move to Santa Fe loomed large and frightening in the forefront of my thoughts. Again, I felt the familiar alienation creep back into my awareness. I felt far away from everything and everyone I had known from my childhood. I wondered then what kind of fulfillment awaited me in the future. My life was one big question mark. I knew it and I didn't like it. It was disconcerting to watch all the building blocks that my life rested upon fall down around me in a sweeping demolition.

What I had been raised to believe I was supposed to have accomplished by now: career, marriage, buying a home, having a family, being "settled," mature, a grown-up had for the most part eluded me. Or, just not brought about inner satisfaction. Instead I was going through a late adolescence, having to find myself all over again at age twenty-eight and nothing at all, especially me, was settled.

Somehow, I motivated myself to roll up my sleeping bag, pack up my tent, and even go for a short hike before Nellie came to get me. The fresh air and movement of my body warmed me up. The blood pulsing through my aching limbs brought new life moving through my veins and cleared my head.

As I walked along the trail I had hiked the evening before, the sun was just beginning to warm the rocks. I asked myself as I walked if I was really moving to Santa Fe as the result of some kind of vision I had had the night before. The answer that came back to me from deep inside was a resounding, "Yes. Of course."

I was beginning to sound like Nellie to myself, I thought wryly. I had managed to make an otherworldly experience seem matter of fact and commonplace. But it rang true for me that my next course of action was to move to Santa Fe and to begin a life there. It seemed perfectly logical.

By the time I saw Nellie's van rolling down the dirt

road toward me, stirring up huge clouds of dust, I felt calm enough to be able to tell her what I had experienced the night before.

Nellie looked tired as she got out of her van and walked toward me. It was a long trip for her, here and back, twice on my behalf. A smile lit up her face when she saw me. She waved and I waved back, returning the smile.

Nellie was not like my mother who would want to know everything that had happened immediately and would ask question after question to cover all bases. Nellie hugged me lightly and looked into my eyes. I looked back full on. I had no secrets from her.

"Looks like you're ready to go," she said at last.

"Yup," I answered. "I had a pretty interesting night," I volunteered.

"I knew you would, Sara," she said quietly.

As I put my tent, sleeping bag, and backpack into her van, we made small talk. Nellie, it seemed had predicted the outcome of my vision quest and was not at all surprised by anything I told her about my experience.

As we bounced down twisting, dirt roads in Nellie's van with the bad shock absorbers, Nellie smiled her wise smile and her eyes lit up.

"Sara, that's wonderful," she said finally, tossing her wiry hair back off her lined face as I told her of my decision to return to Santa Fe to live.

The drive back to Nellie's adobe house, the evening spent talking and having dinner with Nellie and her kids, the deep sleep I had in Kate's room all seemed to pass by in a blur. I was warm and fed and loved. My cold night alone in the wilderness with an empty stomach was behind me. It was a little triumph but one worth paying attention to, I thought. I knew more difficulties lay ahead, however, and wanted to put them out of my mind for one more night before going back to Colorado and to Michael.

The morning of my departure, I headed out right after breakfast. The kids were off to school and Nellie was off to run errands. I was going back to Boulder. I felt a knot in my stomach as I said goodbye to Nellie.

"I just don't know how all this is going to play out," I told her as we stood outside in her driveway.

"Of course, you don't," Nellie said. "If we knew how everything was going to turn out, we wouldn't be fully alive.

"Living is about being fully in the mystery and trusting the outcome," she added.

I was tired and apprehensive as I got into my car and drove away from the warmth of Nellie's kindness and onto the highway going north.

Driving back home to Boulder from Santa Fe allowed me time to think about my vision. I felt then that my night alone in the mountains had cemented my destiny to the desert land where I pitched my tent.

I had never belonged anywhere, but I knew then that I belonged in northern New Mexico. I knew then that I would return—it was my destiny.

But first, I had to convince Michael to come with me. And that wasn't going to be easy.

CHASING THE AFTERGLOW

Nature is ever at work building and pulling down, creating and destroying, keeping everything whirling and flowing, allowing no rest but in rhythmical motion, chasing everything in endless song out of one beautiful form into another.

~ John Muir

When I got home late that evening, Michael was at work. He was a waiter at a European-style bistro. I laughed to myself about this. Michael had never been a waiter before. He had mainly done construction in Belgium. And he played classical piano. But ever the charmer, Michael had gotten hired at a coveted Boulder eatery using his gift of gab and unnerving fearlessness. The restaurant was formal, requiring finesse and knowledge of fine dining etiquette. Michael was a complete novice. Yet, he put on his white starched shirt and bluffed his way through. And, miraculously, he did well. He pulled the whole thing off without a hitch.

I went to bed and lay awake, awaiting his arrival home with a twinge of longing, coupled with anxious anticipation. Should I or shouldn't I talk to him about what had happened in Santa Fe? If I were to broach the subject, I might get shot down immediately and, given the seriousness of this decision, that would be awful. I had to be cautious, feel things out first, I decided. This was too important to approach casually.

Michael could be moody. He did not buy into all the spiritual stuff I was into and certainly did not appreciate Nellie's influence in my life. The two of them, while acquainted, hardly ever spoke. They seemed to be competing for different pieces of me; Michael for my body and Nellie for my soul.

I decided to play it by ear and see how things shook out when I saw him.

Before too long, I heard Michael enter the house, walk into the kitchen, and open the refrigerator. Apparently, as was his habit, he was getting something to eat before bed. Working late, Michael always took a while to wind down before he got tired enough to sleep.

Since he did not rush straight into the bedroom to welcome me home, I got up, wrapped my robe around me, and cautiously went to greet him.

"Hi," he said casually. He came up and hugged me. It was a lukewarm hug at best. I faintly smelled liquor on his breath. Michael liked to hang around after his shift and party with the wait staff. He was completely in his element with the free high-end drinks and a ready-made party every night.

"How was your trip?" he asked mechanically, appearing disinterested. Michael's vibe was more pretense than real. He kept his emotions in check most of the time.

"Great," I said with a smile. I sensed his distance with an ache in my gut. The all-too-familiar wall that Michael had around his emotions and, lately, even his body, kept me at arm's length. I didn't address it.

Michael seated himself at the kitchen table and ate his peanut butter sandwich. I sat down directly across from him and looked him straight in the eye.

"You've been drinking," I said abruptly and then immediately regretted it. Michael frowned and averted his gaze.

"You know it helps me unwind from a busy shift," he said briskly.

I sighed and said nothing. The conversation was finished. We sat facing each other in silence for a few minutes, neither one of us trying to fill the distance between us.

Sadly, this emotional lake separating us was becoming status quo. This was how things were, I said to myself with melancholy resignation. I should just go back to bed. But I sat frozen in time and space for a minute, just looking around.

Everything in our home belonged to me. Michael had nothing when he moved in and was content to live in "my" house, which all of a sudden seemed strange.

I made myself a cup of chamomile tea. We seem so normal, I thought then; just an ordinary young couple at home together, having a midnight snack. Actually, it was past midnight. The clock on the stove said 1:52.

Michael finished eating and, without a word, sulked into the living room and settled into the couch. He turned on the TV and began surfing channels methodically with the remote, putting his feet up on the coffee table and opening a beer he had grabbed from the refrigerator on his way out of the kitchen.

His indifference was meant to punish me for bringing up a taboo subject: Michael's drinking. I went over to the frayed beige couch and cuddled up beside him, resting my head on his shoulder affectionately. I decided to try after all.

"I'm happy to see you," I said.

Michael did look at me then, tenderly, for a second.

"You too," he said obligingly.

He kissed me and gave my hand a quick squeeze and turned back to the TV.

"I'll see you soon," I whispered. "I'm exhausted after my long drive."

Truthfully, I was somewhat relieved that I didn't have to deal with him. I wasn't ready to talk to him about Santa Fe. There would be plenty of time to talk in the morning, I reasoned. Besides, I was too tired to think straight.

Our bedroom furniture, of course, was mine—unmatched dressers, a queen-sized bed with a quilted bedspread on it from my single days—white with light green and soft pink flowers. Michael had said he didn't mind so I didn't bother to replace it.

I lay down on my side of the bed. We were living separate lives. We had become roommates, in spite of all the passion we'd experienced at the beginning.

I had already done the unthinkable: I had married Michael. Even before that, we endured an on-again, off-again relationship that would go smoothly for a period of time then would be interrupted by one or another crisis, usually having to do with Michael's either falling for another woman or having to return to Belgium when his tourist visa ran out.

On my end, this made for a great deal of angst and heartache. I knew intellectually that no man was ever going to complete me. Yet, I couldn't separate myself from Michael. It was just not something I had the stomach to do. I really didn't understand why.

At one point after having just returned from an extended time away, Michael popped the question. After thinking about it for about two seconds, I agreed to marry him. We were in my tiny apartment in Manhattan. It was a year after we had met in the reggae club. I was twenty-five. Michael was living in Brooklyn with a group of guys. All my friends were getting married. I didn't want to be the last old maid standing. Besides, I was crazy about Michael then.

His proposal, if it could be called that, seemed spontaneous. We were lying together locked in an afternoon embrace on my bed, having just had incredible sex. It was the product of desperation born of months calling and writing to each other while Michael tried to get his tourist visa renewed. It took a lot longer than he had anticipated.

I was terrified Michael would not make it back. And yet, here he was, finally. We were together at last and I didn't want to lose him.

"It would be so much easier for us to be together if we were married," Michael had whispered.

Shocked, I inhaled sharply, pulling away a little to look at him. Cars honked loudly outside on the street. It was rush hour.

Michael met my gaze and stroked my hair. "I mean it," he said softly.

"Okay," I said. "I'll marry you."

"Really?" Michael asked, gazing into my hazel eyes with his own. Our eyes were exactly the same color.

"Yes," I said.

It wasn't a proposal, but I took it as such. Michael had needed to find a way to stay in the country. He loved it here. I knew he loved me too. We loved each other. Yet, it wasn't the kind of enduring love that good marriages are made of. It was young, obsessive love. Crazy love. A love that brings with it longing and desperation as much as it brings pleasure.

A few hours later, after Michael had left for his apartment, my decision sent me reeling. How could I do it? How could I not do it? I hadn't yet learned to love myself. Michael's love, in spite of the fact that it was second best, was better than no love at all, I had felt at the time. And, without Michael, I feared there would be no one to fill the dark and ominous void in my heart.

I had moved to New York to finish my bachelor's degree, which I did, and to work as a massage therapist. While the city was fun and exciting, its intensity did not agree with my sensitive nervous system. I wanted to get back to Colorado, where I had gone to massage school and where I still had friends.

After Michael and I decided to get married, I gave up my apartment in New York and he and I and went to live in Boulder.

We got married six months later in a simple non-denominational ceremony in the mountains. Michael and I exchanged vows in the presence of a New Age minister and two friends. Throughout the brief and simple ceremony, I knew deep down I was marrying Michael for the wrong reasons.

While charming to a fault at his best, at his worst Michael was a con artist, a player, a womanizer, and a flirt. All of this I came to know about Michael within the first months of our involvement. Yet, rather than deter me from desiring him, his shortcomings fueled my desire even more. And, like pouring gasoline on a fire, the more Michael came on strong then retreated, as was his tendency, the more determined I was to make him stay with me for good.

Compelled to go deeper and deeper into my involvement with Michael, I was completely unable to comprehend that one could have feelings for another that were as strong as mine were for him without behaving rashly. I had been in over my head since our first meeting.

As I lay in bed, waiting for my husband of three years, maybe I was coming to the surface of reality. But I wasn't ready to fully embrace it yet. Even though I wasn't aware of it at the time, I just wanted to pretend to myself a little bit longer that Michael and I were destined for happily ever after.

I fell asleep before Michael came to bed. In the morning I got up early for work, being careful not to wake him. I tiptoed around the bedroom, gathering my clothes, thankful that the precious secret of my time in Santa Fe and my decision to move there was tucked safely away inside my memory. Michael stirred in his sleep; I left quickly, carefully closing the bedroom door behind me.

I didn't want to deal with a possible hangover, which I knew from experience could turn his silence from the night before into grumpiness and even meanness. Michael had a cruel streak in him with words that could wound. Once early on in our relationship, Michael had told me he was in love with someone else: one of the women who hung around his house in Brooklyn. It was a guy house, a party house, there were always people in and out, artists, punk rock musicians and, naturally, lots of women coming and going. She was among them.

I had been devastated but Michael had no tolerance for my feelings. After determining that she didn't share his feelings, Michael had come back to me. He refused to discuss with me what had transpired between them, dismissing me abruptly if I ever chose to bring it up. I stopped asking after a short while.

I'd fallen into the habit of not communicating with him so, I reasoned it was best to go on about my day without mentioning a possible move. When had I gotten so accustomed to walking on eggshells, I asked myself.

It took a couple of days before I was brave enough to broach the subject. We were sitting outside on the patio of a local Tex-Mex place eating chips and salsa and drinking beer. He seemed relaxed and happy, for once, even engaged, so I decided the time had come to fill Michael in on Santa Fe.

"So, I had a really interesting time down in Santa Fe visiting Nellie," I said. "Would you like to hear about it?"

A faint flicker of annoyance crossed his face. "Sure."

I took a deep breath and pushed on. "I spent some time alone in the wilderness and really fell in love with the land," I ventured.

Michael just stared at me evenly, taking another sip of beer. He certainly would rather people-watch on the Pearl Street Mall instead of have a serious conversation. It was a beautiful evening, sunny and not too hot. As was typical, the Mall was teeming with visitors, families, wannabe musicians playing guitars for donations, an assortment of aging hippies, well-to-do Baby Boomers, and college students.

"It is really beautiful there and Nellie thinks it would be a great place for us to live—all kinds of healing arts stuff going on and it's pretty hip, kind of like the Aspen of New Mexico.

I wasn't going to go down the spiritual road with Michael. He wouldn't get the vision quest or the vision itself. I didn't even want to try. I hemmed and hawed. I almost lost my nerve completely but somehow pressed on.

"Look, I really want us to move there," I blurted out. "I fell in love with everything about it. I'm dying to go back."

Michael grinned widely. "That's great," he said. "What took you so long to tell me?"

Relief flowed through me like a wave. "I was scared you wouldn't want to move," I said.

"You know I'm always up for a new adventure," Michael said. And he was right. He always was. He had gladly followed me to Boulder from New York three years earlier, so why not Santa Fe now? In my insecurity about the state of our relationship, I was overlooking the obvious: Michael was on a grand adventure. He was living in the U.S. and married to a young woman who liked to be on the move.

He and I shared a love of travel. He was not so concerned about who he was with but where he was going. I provided him with a means to see the country, meet interesting people, live in a variety of places. He was not about to turn that down.

Interestingly enough, as we planned our move to Santa Fe, Michael talked more and more about wanting to give his own business a try. As was typical of my relationship with Michael, it soon became murky which one of us was getting the better deal. I had gotten my way in regard to the move to Santa Fe. He, on the other hand, had used this as a bargaining chip to get me to agree to his business venture. In our usual unclear state, we made plans to move at the end of the summer.

We packed up our small apartment with little fanfare. We lived minimally in a rented condo, acquiring most of our possessions, like pots, pans, bowls, plates, kitchen utensils, even small pieces of furniture, coffee tables, etc., from thrift stores and yard sales.

We sorted through our things. We had everything we needed to live simply but comfortably, I told myself as our packing progressed. Yet, I wondered if we really did have what it would take to make it in Santa Fe as a married couple.

While I was excited to be moving to Santa Fe and making a change, I simply enjoyed the diversion of packing and the activity that it created. It was something Michael and I could do together. I began to entertain hope that we would actually be okay once we got there. I fantasized that a fresh start would heal our floundering relationship.

Since Michael worked nights as a waiter and I worked afternoons and evenings as a massage therapist, we spent our mornings tying up loose ends and running errands getting ready for our move. In spite of the togetherness I had envisioned, we each spent a certain amount of time packing alone.

I found myself thinking back to my first-ever crush. The intensity of my feelings at the tender age of eight reminded me of how strongly I had felt about Michael at the beginning.

That was the time my family lived in Riverside, California, for a year. It was quite a departure from suburban life, as we lived at the end of a cul-de-sac, bordering rolling desert-like hills and surrounded by open space. I loved to play hide-and-seek at dusk with the neighborhood kids. There were lots of large rocks and dry hills made from mounds of dirt to hide behind. I loved the wild feeling I had as I ran with all my might, breathing cool evening air in the approaching twilight. It was behind one of these mounds of dirt that I experienced my first kiss.

Robbie was the son of my parents' friends. Both sets of parents were university professors. Our family and his got together frequently for dinner. With my younger brother and sister and Robbie's two brothers, we formed a pack of six kids. Running wildly around the yard, we would laugh and play tag and chase. My favorite game was hide-and-seek, best played at dusk.

One such evening, while in the middle hide-and-seek, Robbie and I found ourselves alone, far from the others. We hid behind a huge rock and huddled close together. An evening chill filled the air. Suddenly, Robbie said, "I love you, Sara," and then we kissed almost imperceptibly. It was so light and quick that I wondered if I had dreamt it. But I knew it had really happened and my life had been forever changed.

I soared over the hillside in absolute joyous disbelief. I was loved. I had been kissed.

My family moved away shortly afterwards, and Robbie and I lost touch. But that feeling I had of everything being so wonderful and shiny after being kissed remained with me. It was something I kept chasing like a crack addict, forever craving the rush of the first hit, with every subsequent deep inhale of drugs never quite hitting the mark.

Somewhere in the back of my mind, I knew I was addicted to Michael. But I wasn't ready to admit it to myself yet.

Finally, the big day arrived. Michael and I were Santa Fe bound. We had each given notice at our jobs, told our landlord that we were leaving the condo, and I had excitedly informed Nellie about our imminent arrival. She was less enthusiastic about Michael coming with me. She had a premonition of what was going to happen and was somewhat flat about it.

As we packed our boxes into the rented U-Haul, it was still early in the day.

"It sucks to move in August," Michael said to me as he wiped his sweaty hands on his shorts.

"I know," I replied, rolling my eyes at him and pretending a sigh.

Michael was right. We had hitched one of the cars to the U-Haul truck, and I was going to drive the other one that was so full of stuff that I couldn't see out the back window. We were going to ride as a caravan, following each other down and maybe stopping halfway there for a picnic.

"Let's do it," he said with a grin. "Santa Fe, here we come."

I hugged Michael. "Thanks for doing this with me," I said.

"I've never been to New Mexico, so why not?" Michael said matter-of-factly.

I got into my little red Toyota Tercel and, map on the passenger seat, started the engine, headed toward the parking lot exit and pulling over into an empty space. I was waiting while Michael circled the unwieldy truck and car swung out onto the road.

I followed him. This was because he was going slower

than me and so we could stay together this way.

I had always loved road trips. Long-distance driving appealed to me because I liked having uninterrupted time to think and daydream. This day was no different. The solitude of the road, the dry heat of August, the uncertainty of what lay ahead all lured me into a kind of trance-like state where I concentrated on where I was going and on following Michael in the trailer, but I did not let myself panic.

I loved the mountainous landscape that we passed through and I let myself just be in the moment. Time alone would tell what would appear on the horizon.

The first time I lived in the Rocky Mountains I was eighteen years old, ten years prior.

After spending a year at a liberal arts college in Amherst, Massachusetts, I traveled to Colorado for the summer. For kids growing up on the East Coast like myself, going out West after high school or during summer vacations from college was a popular rite of passage. For me, the brief trip West would turn out to be a lifetime move, but I didn't know it at the time.

I had found a ride to Colorado on the university ride-board, sharing the drive with a woman who was bound for Aspen. I spent the summer in Bailey, a little mountain town nestled in a valley, a steep, fertile stretch of land, sandwiched between two mountain peaks, about 100 miles west of Denver. There, I found a waitressing job at a resort.

With my friend, another waitress named Annie who was originally from Minnesota, I hitchhiked to Glenwood Springs during one weekend off. We rode with a couple of ranchers who only had space in the back of their pick-up truck.

As we approached Glenwood Canyon, Annie and I lay on our backs in the bed of the truck and observed the intricate canyon walls upside down and from a speed of seventy miles per hour. The colorful rock formations blurred together like fudge swirls in vanilla ice cream being stirred slowly. The layers of dark slate and light granite looked delicious as we sped past.

This had been my introduction to the West and I had been drawn to the land ever since. Now, I was driving away from the Rocky Mountains but still felt happy. I looked at the wispy clouds, the green forests. As we approached New Mexico, I observed a flattening and softening of the landscape. New Mexico was dryer than Colorado and more open. Not a single cloud was in the sky as we approached Santa Fe. It was dusk but still light. The afterglow was gorgeous.

As Michael pulled over at a Holiday Inn at the outskirts of town, I said to myself, "I'm almost home."

We would spend the night there and the following day would go house hunting.

My legs hurt and my head ached. I was dusty and thirsty from the road. Michael got out of his vehicle in front of me, stood up and arched his back in a slow backward stretch. He came over to my car and, as I rolled down the window, said with a grin, "Let's go get some dinner."

GEOGRAPHICAL FIX
IN THE HIGH-ALTITUDE DESERT

If you don't like something, change it. If you can't change it, change your attitude.

~ Maya Angelou

The next morning was hot and dry. Michael and I woke still exhausted from the road trip. I could see the sun, already too bright from our hotel room. We checked out quickly and ate breakfast at an authentic New Mexico-style diner. The worn tables were partially covered with small Mexican blankets running down the center as decorations. Dusty ristras, small bunches of dried red chilies, hung in the center of the windows.

I felt so strange I didn't know whether to laugh or cry. I looked up at Michael for some sense of what he was feeling but his eyes were fixed on the menu.

We each ordered huevos rancheros and the green chile was so hot I had to gulp down ice water after each bite.

"This is the real deal, I guess," Michael said, inhaling through pursed lips to cool the heat.

"Amazing," I answered. "I've never eaten anything like this first thing in the morning."

We laughed through our first breakfast in Santa Fe. It seemed better than going the melancholy route, I decided. Then we went house hunting.

I had envisioned a cute little adobe cottage in a beautiful setting, maybe surrounded by trees. As the day progressed and the sun got more and more oppressive, my hopes dimmed in equal measure.

At six o'clock that evening we ended up renting a 1970s, ranch-style three bedroom in a middle-class enclave just north of town. The neighborhood was dotted with small non-descript homes with aluminum siding and parched yards, devoid of anything green and living. Realistically, it was all we could afford.

We didn't do anything to celebrate. Too tired to unpack or even speak much, Michael and I pulled our sleeping bags in from the U-Haul and slept on the living room floor. I was grateful to be inside somewhere and off the road.

The next day I felt raw. My body ached from sleeping on a hard surface. The house seemed drab and ordinary. What was I thinking in coming here, I wondered as I unpacked our things. Emotionless, I unloaded the kitchen, the bedroom, and the bathroom. For the first time since I had gone on the vision quest six months prior, I felt afraid.

I was unused to the light in northern New Mexico. But I began to understand why artists flocked to the area. Everything around me seemed illuminated, stark, jarring. The high altitude, thin atmosphere, absence of tall trees or buildings all added to the sense of being far away from anything known. I was in unfamiliar territory. There was nowhere to hide.

Michael and I had to unload the U-Haul right away so he could return it to the Santa Fe office and retrieve our deposit. In spite of the heat and disorientation, we worked together in robotic fashion until everything was out of the trailer and in a pile inside the house.

I followed Michael out to the U-Haul drop off and then we rode back together to our new home. Almost immediately I sensed something was wrong. Neither of us seemed very upbeat. I noticed how the same dynamic that played itself out between us in Boulder was still there: Michael withdrawing and me afraid or unwilling to fish him out into the open. It seemed like too much effort as we rode home that morning.

We passed the quaint downtown plaza: an enclosed green space surrounded with picturesque adobe buildings. Then we headed south, toward our suburban home. Everything was flat and dry. It seemed to me that life, as I had previously known it, had disappeared into the heat and wide landscape.

I turned up the air conditioner, but it was already on high. I fiddled with the radio and only succeeded in tuning into an AM talk show. Nothing really earth-shattering, so I turned it off.

"So, here we are," I said to Michael finally. "We're stranded in a strange city, know virtually no one, and both of us need work."

"Yeah," Michael replied. "This is nothing new for me. I've been living like this since I came to the States for the first time four years ago."

It was true. Michael was a traveler, heart and soul. He flourished in these types of situations. I, on the other hand, for the first time in my life was seeking stability.

Michael had not changed since we had first met. I was the one who had changed. I was getting older, growing up, realizing that not everything about my past was so bad that I had to become the opposite of what my parents and the adults around me had wanted for me.

When I was younger, I never questioned the path my life would take: high school, college, beginning a professional life, a happy marriage, kids... summer vacations, a comfortable middle-class income without ever having to experience much financial hardship.

But an inner restlessness that I couldn't shake overtook me at the age of eighteen, after my first year of college that changed the course of my life dramatically.

It was during that year that I planned my ticket out. I found a summer job in Colorado, found a ride out west on the ride board and took off for parts unknown.

Again, for many kids growing up in the northeast, myself included, going out west after high school or during college vacations was a popular rite of passage. For me, the brief trip west turned out to be a lifetime move, but I didn't know it at the time. Once I had made it out to Colorado, there was no turning back.

I lived and worked in a small town in the Rocky Mountains, west of Denver and took off traveling to California the following summer. By the time I had reached age twenty, I had found my way to Boulder, Colorado, where I enrolled in the Boulder School of Massage Therapy.

I remember clearly my letter home, "Dear Mom and Dad, I have decided to pursue my interest in the healing arts by enrolling in the Boulder School of Massage Therapy. This decision has precipitated my dropping out of college and remaining in Colorado."

In other words, I would not be coming home ever again.

Doing things my way was what I had decided to do, and it included marrying Michael and moving with him to

Santa Fe. Truthfully, I had realized by then I didn't know what the hell I was doing. But, there was no turning back. I'll just have to figure things out on my own, I thought. Relying upon my wits was my habitual way of living and had been for a long, long time.

As our early days in Santa Fe unfolded, I settled into the task of job hunting. I had been previously been warned by well-meaning friends that Santa Fe was not a promising place to find work. Furthermore, the rents were high, and wages were low. I found these facts to be true.

After about two weeks, I finally got a job as a massage therapist at a resort twenty miles south of town. I loved the gorgeous drive out there; however, the work was sporadic. When I interviewed, which entailed giving the resort owner a massage, she told me there was a rumor circulating among the staff that the place was built on top of ancient Native American burial grounds. It seemed to be an odd topic for a first meeting, never mind a job interview.

It turned out the staff often spoke about this fact. They used it as a means to justify that, in spite of its beauty and prime location on a pristine mesa overlooking miles and miles of spacious sagebrush-dotted hills, the resort was never booked to capacity. There was never enough business to keep the place financially solvent or its personnel gainfully employed.

To make matters worse, Michael and I had to get a roommate simply to be able to afford the rent on our relatively mediocre house. After interviewing a host of unconventional characters, we decided on someone stable: a high school teacher and coach of the local high school football team.

He occupied the master bedroom and adjoining bathroom, sharing the common areas and kitchen. Essentially, we lived with a stranger who came and went as he pleased, compromising our privacy.

Eventually, Michael got a loan for his business and spent long hours renovating a delivery truck, turning it into a traditional Belgian "french-fry" stand. His plan was to sell homemade fresh fries with a variety of sauces. These trucks are found all over Belgium, he reasoned, so why not try it in the States?

Because I was trying to get adjusted to a new town and Michael and I were not really plugged in yet with activities and friends, I was afforded the dubious luxury to ponder the rhetorical question, "How did I get here?"

I had lived a very ordinary life. I had experienced nothing highly traumatic in my childhood. Yet, I often felt like I didn't belong in my family, in my school, in my town. I was always a little off-center, just a bit out of touch, kind of a spaced-out kid, even before I started smoking pot.

While my parents had truly wanted the best for me, they were overly concerned with outward appearances and either unwilling or unable to pay attention to any inner issues that I was dealing with. I learned early on that as long as I appeared okay, everyone was happy. If I did have a problem, it was best to keep it to myself.

This was my marriage in a nutshell. Michael and I didn't talk. He was fine. I was hurting and as long as I didn't bring it up, everything else was fine too. If we seemed okay on the outside, that was what mattered.

By the time I had met Michael, four years before we moved to Santa Fe together, I had been through some uncertain times. I had wanted to put all that behind me then by the simple act of falling in love. I was engaging in something called magical thinking, I realized years later.

Bound together by our strained and strange matrimony, we began to explore Santa Fe's beckoning maze of possibilities. Because Santa Fe is a mecca for a wide variety of fringe societal elements, just walking around downtown was an adventure.

Santa Fe represents a convergence of three distinct cultures: Anglo, Latino, and Native American. Coupled with its unique ecology and climate, renowned northern New Mexico cuisine, trademark adobe architecture and famed outdoor opera house, Santa Fe was a rich place for me to be.

I was thrilled with everything I saw, curious, open, and taking in everything like a breath of fresh air. I felt like I was living in a foreign country sometimes while wandering through Santa Fe. To me, the place was brand new.

I found myself in a local bookstore one afternoon. There was a bulletin board in the back advertising what seemed like a million different healing modalities, gatherings, and lectures.

There were flyers for psychics, bodyworkers, herbalists, channelers, crystal enthusiasts, animal communicators, acupuncturists (there are two acupuncture colleges in Santa Fe), massage therapists, spiritual teachers, past-life regressionists, hypnotherapists, gurus, naturopaths and homeopaths, just to name a few. The City Different, as Santa Fe was aptly known, was home to a surprising wealth of healers, both legitimate and questionable. I felt as euphoric as a kid in a candy store. I could take my pick!

I flashed back briefly to my night alone in the desert where I heard the call to come to Santa Fe. This was a place for spiritual seekers, and I was here seeking. I felt a surge of goosebumps. Was I drawn here for a reason? I had a moment of clarity. Whatever it was I was seeking, I was not alone in my search. Others were on this path too and here, in the bookstore, I had found proof.

Unfortunately, this lightness I had felt didn't last long. I had become habituated to thinking negatively about myself. I was a chronic worrier and living with Michael provided plenty of fuel for the fire of my angst.

For example, he and I were wandering near the capitol one afternoon and got entirely immersed in Native American jewelry. Members of nearby pueblos regularly came to sell their wares along the "plaza," a central square blocked off to cars. Swarming with tourists and locals alike, crowds thronged to purchase handmade, traditional turquoise and silver rings, belt buckles, necklaces, and bracelets for bargain prices.

I watched, enthralled, realizing that may families came into town from the pueblos for the day, selling wares a few times a month that they and others had hand-crafted. This was how they made their living.

Often, there would be three generations mulling around a chaotic scene on the sidewalk, where the wares were spread out on blankets. Kids with runny noses stayed close to their mothers' sides, while fathers or grandparents haggled with potential buyers.

The Indians were dirt poor. They dressed in thrift store clothing and ate their lunches of fry bread and pinto beans from plastic sacks they brought with them for the day. In spite of being surrounded by more than a dozen trendy restaurants along the plaza, that aspect of Santa Fe was off-limits to them. It was tough to see.

"Let's see if we can pick up a large amount of this stuff at a discount," Michael said to me, eyeing the assorted rings, bracelets, key chains, and other jewelry spread out all around us like he was casing the joint.

"I bet we could make a fortune selling this stuff to my family and friends in Belgium."

I got upset.

"How can you think about that when these people are barely scraping by?" I asked.

"Look, that's not my problem," Michael snapped back. "It would be a huge hit in Europe, I just know it."

I was worried Michael was going to start bargaining on the spot to see how much merchandise he could buy with the least amount of money.

"Okay," I said. "But if you use the money you got for your business loan to buy jewelry, how will you be able to start the business?"

Michael grumbled something about waiting a few days before investing in mass quantities of jewelry and contacting his brother in Belgium about going in on a joint business venture.

At least Michael didn't embarrass me on the spot. But, the interaction left me feeling disturbed. I was deeply touched by the humility of the jewelry makers. The way they embraced their traditional craft with pride was meaningful to me. They had earned my respect.

Michael, on the other hand, was ready to jump in and exploit them for his personal gain. What the hell was I doing with this guy anyway? I wondered to myself. I had no answer.

One day, I returned from a particularly slow morning at the resort feeling very frustrated. In four hours of hanging around there, I had only done one massage. I did get a ten-dollar tip and I did get to soak in one of the hot tubs for free, I told myself, but that seemed like small consolation.

Then the phone rang.

"Sara," Nellie said in her usual no-nonsense tone, "I want you to call and make an appointment with a shaman I know of."

I sighed. Nellie was always well informed about the various new-age goings-on. Although I did not see her every day or even every week because we were both occupied with the details of our very different lives, she would call and inform me about a particular event or person from time to time that I "just had to check out."

She said this man was an honest-to-goodness shaman who was living up in the mountains that I just had to see. He was receiving people on his land, she said, and doing some sort of healing ceremony with them.

I was beginning to trust in her quirkiness and also to feel a little desperate for some guidance about my new life.

"Who is this guy and how soon can I go see him?" I asked immediately.

She said she didn't want to talk too much about Martin, the shaman, over the phone.

"Come over and have some tea with me and let's catch up a little first," Nellie said.

When I hung up the phone, I felt relieved. In spite of the fact that Michael and I had been living in Santa Fe for a little over a month, this was my first invitation to Nellie's house since we had arrived in town.

A couple of days later I found myself driving up the familiar driveway that led to Nellie's comfortable home. Finally, I said to myself, a chance to relax in the company of a good friend.

I arrived at her house in the afternoon. As usual, we were seated at her kitchen table drinking bancha tea and eating fresh homemade tortillas with butter and honey.

As they were accustomed, her three cats lay curled up on the table, forming a centerpiece. Beside them were dried flowers in a vase, discarded petals strewn all over the muslin tablecloth. I began to wind down. Her home was so cozy.

I sat down at the kitchen table. "I'm not getting anywhere with my life goals," I complained.

"Plus, I feel confused about what to do," I continued. "I feel like I'm stuck in taffy with no motivation to pull myself out of it and take some focused action."

Nellie was silent for a full minute. Sunshine poured into her adobe-walled kitchen. I cradled my tea and took a bite of tortilla, a buttery-honey blur.

Nellie shooed the cats off the table. "I'm really glad you are going to see my medicine man friend, Martin," Nellie said, leaning back in her cushioned chair next to mine.

"I don't want to say too much about Martin before you meet him yourself," Nellie said. "What I can say for sure is that this guy is for real and what he is tapping into is very deep."

In hindsight, I'm not certain why I trusted Nellie so totally to guide me through the labyrinth of spiritual growth I was negotiating. She was more than just a casual friend, not quite a family member. I came to view her as a something like a guardian angel who knew what to say or not to, and in this way, she earned my trust little by little until I had few doubts.

Of course, as I was agreeing to go see this shaman, the skeptic in me began to have doubts about what I was doing and why. Simply because Nellie told me to do something, I was going along with it without a single clue about what I was getting myself into.

Yet, remembering the powerful experience of my vision quest, which Nellie had initiated, and which had led me to move to Santa Fe with Michael, I decided to go along with another one of her unconventional, if not downright zany suggestions.

Several days later I rose before dawn and drove the fifteen miles out of town to the rural dwelling place of Martin, self-proclaimed medicine man, and his family. I left Michael curled up in bed, mumbling a startled good bye. Obviously, he knew I was going someplace, but I didn't want to say too much. It was early October by this time and a thick, cold fog hung above the city, locked in underneath the mountains like a white parka.

As I was about half a mile from Martin's land, I saw horses grazing along the roadside, silently chewing on cool grass. Several distinct trails of smoke then caught my eye. As I pulled into the clearing, I soon saw three dwellings, two teepees and a small log cabin, with smoke rising from their chimneys.

I began to get nervous all of a sudden as I thought of Michael sleeping soundly and wondered why I didn't have the sense to just stay in bed beside him. But the sun was rising and light was filling the sky. An opaque white canopy seemed to cover my surroundings with a dusting of hope.

Martin, a round, bearded man with matted red hair and bright blue eyes came out of one of the teepees and waved at me and, coming to greet me as I got out of the car.

"Hi. Nice to see you," he said as he held out his hand to shake mine.

"Nice to meet you too," I said. "I'm Sara."

Martin snorted. It was a half laugh that signified, "I know who you are." But then also let me know he wasn't one for small talk and in his world, introductions really weren't all that necessary.

Walking back to the teepee, he pulled the flap back and motioned me inside.

I followed him, ducking to get inside the teepee's entrance.

Then I sat quietly by his pot-bellied wood stove, the teepee smelling of smoke, unsure what was going to happen next.

Martin took his time filling me in.

"First we're going to sit down and drink some tea together," he said. "We're going to chat a bit and get to know each other a little before I read the stones for you."

Martin heated water in a blackened kettle on the stove. Tea was made, and we drank as he surveyed me. I must have appeared bewildered and stone-faced, a woman from New England who was living in Santa Fe who felt the need to consult with a medicine man early one morning.

"I have been reading stones for a long time now," Martin said. "My father-in-law, a native Guatemalan shaman, trained me in his tradition. I came back here to the states to help people like yourself."

"Oh," was all I could get out of my mouth.

I looked around the round space, muddy and unkempt. Martin and his young family were definitely living off the land, I thought. Stacks of plastic containers held rice, beans, and other staples.

Piles of blankets lay neatly folded in one area and kitchen utensils, bowls, and some pots lay in another. Everything, including Martin himself, looked like it needed a good scrubbing.

As I surveyed his living space, I nearly bolted. But I willed myself to keep calm. Sensing my unease, Martin caught my eye and winked at me.

"Let me tell you a little about myself before we get started," he said gently.

I was immediately relieved. I definitely wanted to know more about this odd person before I could surrender my skepticism.

"I'm an American, just like you, but I was partially raised on a Pueblo reservation nearby. I traveled to Guatemala as a young man, settled in a small village, learned the Mayan language and studied with the Village Shaman who became my father-in-law.

"My family and I came back to the United States for safety reasons and I realized a lot of people here can benefit from what I was taught.

"I don't care much for pretenses," he added. "Nor am I a stellar housekeeper, but I've been told I'm a pretty decent shaman."

I laughed at his last comment. I was warming up to him, finally. The tea, wood-burning stove, comfort of the teepee and Martin's self-disclosure put me at ease.

After my tea was finished, we walked together to the teepee next door to consult with the elders about my circumstances, Martin explained.

Unlike the first teepee, this one was stark, neat and arranged with two cushions that were facing each other. Martin sat on one and motioned for me to sit on the other. I obliged.

"So, what can I do for you?" Martin asked at length, training his eyes on me. His voice was hoarse and deep. He looked gritty in his worn denim and flannel.

"I'm feeling confused and I'm searching for meaning," I told him. "I feel like every day I'm grasping at straws, wanting some certainty, some clarity and there is nothing."

I told Martin then about the move to Santa Fe and about Michael. "I have a relationship that feels flat and emotionless and a job that matters little to me."

I told him about the emptiness that threatened to engulf me that never went away, and yet I had a sincere desire to find and follow my passion wherever it led, a desire to help people, make a difference, listen to my heart, if only I could discern its tiny whisper.

Martin nodded in agreement with everything I said. And seemed not to care or notice as tears trickled from my eyes. At length, he held up his hand, motioning me to be silent.

"Now we will see what's what," Martin said. "Let's go to my sacred space where I do my readings."

We left the big teepee. The day was overcast and chilly. There was no sign of civilization in sight, I observed wearily. Martin led the way into a smaller tent. His medicine tent, he called it.

This teepee was less cluttered but equally muddy. It had the same wood-burning smell, contained a smaller stove and had lots of blankets on the floor for us both to sit on.

Martin then began to prophesize for me using a bag of stones. He would say a prayer, cast the stones from his medicine bag and look at them, put them back into his bag and go through the same thing again.

As he went through this ritual, he chanted softly and melodically just loud enough for me to hear. His eyes were slits in his head. He seemed lost in another place and time, not present at all, simply listening to voices from another dimension.

Martin repeated the ritual of casting stones half a dozen times before he looked at me or spoke to me again.

Coming out of his trance, he focused his eyes on me and began to tell me what the stones had said.

"You will overcome much adversity in your life that stems from your childhood," he said. "I see someone who is blocked for the early part of their life and later learns what being unblocked feels like. The adversity is there for a reason, for without it, you wouldn't be able to experience the feeling of it lifting. You will literally feel like you've been shot out of a cannon. The blocks and limitations that you fight against and experience so acutely today will, one day, vanish."

"Oh," I said. It was the second time that morning that I found myself virtually speechless. "That's a relief."

"Without your past," Martin continued in his deep soothing voice, "you wouldn't have the necessary resistance to proceed with your search. You would be too complacent. There would be no pressure to propel you onward. If everything were easy, you would be content to remain on the surface of things when, in fact, you are destined to help many people with your words."

I lay back on the pillows surrounding me, in awe. Me, help others? But I was tired and hungry and spent. The drive, the unusual circumstances, Martin who was wonderful but actually pretty weird, all contributed to my inability to respond.

I must be desperate, I thought.

But then I realized, I *was* desperate.

Desperate to find meaning in a seemingly random universe; Desperate to find my place within it. Desperate to realize that I had a valuable contribution to make through my own tiny life and desperate to understand what that was—so I could begin.

"Thank you so much," I said to Martin finally.

"There's one more thing," Martin said. "The kind of spirituality I practice here, it's not for everyone."

"What do you mean?" I asked.

"What I mean is this," he continued. "It is possible to live a spiritual life in the city, in the midst of all the hustle and bustle of the marketplace. One doesn't have to retreat into a cave to be spiritual.

"Your path may look vastly different from mine. But you can be just as powerful, if not more so, in your own way."

"Oh," I said one more time.

Martin winked at me again and said, "Don't trust me; see for yourself."

Our session was finished.

As I took my leave, few words were exchanged between Martin and myself. He had come out of his trance-like state and seemed like an ordinary back-to-nature guy, living off the land. The stubble on his chin did not betray the wisdom of the stones that he possessed.

Outside the medicine tent, it began to rain—a cold, snowy drizzle that threatened to get worse.

I paid Martin, a small fortune it seemed—and began the drive home in a deep reverie. I wanted to believe him. I wasn't sure if I could—or should.

I passed the horses grazing peacefully in the cool mist and tried to get a glimpse of the mesas beyond the horizon but everything was white, just like it had been when I had arrived. I had been with Martin for two hours.

I felt spacey and tired when I got home. Michael was gone. Off to the hardware store or something, I thought.

I was glad. I didn't want to talk to anyone. I just wanted a strong cup of coffee and a hot shower. In spite of being bone-tired, I felt strangely peaceful. Martin's joyful countenance had rubbed off on me even if just for an instant.

But I still had to deal with the reality of my life with Michael. None of my stuff I was dealing with had miraculously disappeared.

WHEN ONE DOOR CLOSES, ANOTHER DOOR OPENS

Ah, mastery… What a profoundly satisfying feeling when one finally gets on top of a new set of skills… And then sees the light under the new door those skills can open, even as another door is closing.

~ Gail Sheehy

Just like Nellie figured, when I returned from my visit to the shaman, Michael didn't ask me about it. Whether or not he thought it was weird or he just wasn't interested, I didn't know.

Not surprisingly, Michael and I began to drift apart even more now that the move was over and we had arrived. There were days when we hardly spoke. I knew something was going to have to give, and finally it did.

As Michael spent more and more time working on his new business, sometimes twelve to fourteen hours a day, I realized he was living in his Santa Fe and I was living in mine.

For me Santa Fe meant learning about the history, culture, and multifaceted aspects of this place. Enjoying its ambiance, landscapes, architecture, and food.

For Michael, it was another notch on his belt called "Places I have Lived in America."

One afternoon, the phone rang and a female voice on

the other end of the line asked: "Is Michael around?"

"It's for you," I called.

Inside I was crushed. Who could this be? Then I told myself it was nothing to worry about. I had already been through countless discussions with him over being jealous or suspicious and knew that there was no point in making a scene unless I was willing to follow through on my end, once I gleaned the truth.

Michael didn't make any excuses or say anything to me one way or another as he snatched the phone from my hand and began an inaudible conversation with the woman.

With the telephone cord stretched to its maximum length, he turned his back to me and talked quietly into the hallway, projecting his voice the opposite direction from where I stood busying myself in the kitchen.

I strained to listen. Then I caught myself. How had things spiraled so low between us? I asked myself. I was torn between wanting to hear Michael's conversation and just wanting to pretend this wasn't really happening.

The mysterious woman called the house several more times. She would ask for Michael and I would give him the phone. I didn't say anything to him, and he didn't volunteer any information. We would glare at each other in stony silence and then walk away, neither of us wanting to open the can of worms that was waiting.

We hadn't been intimate for weeks. The routine that we had in Boulder of avoiding each other had simply intensified. One was tired and going to bed early. One was working late. We didn't talk. We didn't cook together or eat together. We stopped making love. I was living with a ghost.

But I was used to that. When I was ten, my family moved to Rhode Island, where I lived until I graduated from high school. I had just entered the fifth grade. It was hard being the new kid. I was quiet. I was shy. I was tiny. I was smart. But, most of all, I was introverted. As I progressed through my last two years of elementary school and entered junior high, my tendency to keep to myself and keep things to myself expanded.

Somewhere during my seventh-grade year I became despondent. I lost my appetite and I felt tightness in my throat and stomach all the time. I couldn't relax. I wasn't feeling okay. I was constantly fighting back tears, for what I couldn't say. Something was wrong but I didn't know what.

I had a hard time with the social aspects of junior high school. My friends from South Road got mixed in with kids from two other elementary schools and, typically enough, there were a lot of cliques. The cheerleaders, the jocks, the popular girls who were neither cheerleaders nor jocks but dated the jocks. The nerds (smart kids who were not athletic), and of course the stoners. I looked around and I figured I would never be a jock. I tried out for cheerleading and didn't make the team.

I tried out for gymnastics and didn't make that team either. I could have gone out for track, but I was too scared to try out for something else. There was no way any of the popular guys would want to date me, of this I was dead certain. After a year or two of not belonging anywhere, I made a conscious decision to join the stoners.

Everybody smoked weed on a regular basis. And so did I. By some miracle I managed to keep my A and B average throughout high school. So, my pot smoking and eventual forays into other drugs and heavy drinking went primarily unnoticed by the adults in my world.

My parents were used to me being quiet. I discovered that my introverted tendencies were fed by my marijuana use. I could be there and not really be there. This checking out became my MO for many years to come. I could be in class but really somewhere else. I could be at the dinner table with my family but not there. I could be kissing a guy but not really kissing him.

And so, I became cut off from myself and far away from others who inhabited my world. It was from this deep inner place of pain and aloneness that I spoke to Michael.

We were sitting across from each other at our rough-hewn pine rectangular table in our large family room. Sliding glass doors occupied the southern wall leading out to our backyard. Bright afternoon sunlight poured into the room where we sat and small sparrows darted around the yard, alighting on barren branches. Everything seemed to be moving in slow motion.

Yes, Santa Fe was a beautiful place. The pristine scene outside was a direct contrast to the ugliness occurring inside the house.

"What is going on?" I begged.

"I don't love you anymore," Michael said softly, deliberately. "I've met someone else."

Everything I had been suppressing broke free. Feelings from childhood, my mother's emotional distance, my father's overbearing attempt to compensate, my running away to find solace, a life of my own, true love, everything tumbled out of me in a single sound.

"No," I wailed. I sprang up out of my chair and

pounded my fist on the hard, unyielding table. Immediately I felt a sharp pain in my right hand. It started to swell.

In the moment I was livid, uncoiled, a child having a tantrum, a woman scorned. I sobbed and hugged myself, hot tears streaming down my face.

Michael was somewhere in my periphery: cold, frozen, backing slowly away.

Summoning strength I didn't realize I possessed, words spilled out of me that could never be taken back.

"If you leave now, don't come back," I said.

I had spent a night out alone in the wilderness. I had left home at eighteen and dropped out of college, finding my way in a strange and unpredictable world. I was strong suddenly, a tree with roots deep in the ground and I was powerful enough to shout my truth.

"Just go," I said.

Michael looked embarrassed but relieved. The lie he was living with me had finally been exposed. It was over. He sauntered out without looking back. I heard his car start and looked out the window as he pulled out of the driveway.

There was dead silence in the house. I walked from room to room in a daze. I don't know what I was looking for.

My marriage was in shambles; I had no real income to speak of, a big house to fill with more roommates just to be able to afford the rent. A dream of beginning a new life in Santa Fe turned into a nightmare in a few short months. I spiraled into despair.

I needed to call Nellie. But I knew she wouldn't be surprised. She wouldn't come right out and say, "I told you so," but Nellie could be pretty tough. She wasn't someone to go to for coddling. I couldn't deal with her right then. Besides, my hand was starting to throb.

I got into the car and went directly to the emergency room. Sobbing uncontrollably, I entered the hospital.

I walked down a long corridor that smelled of antiseptic. How did I get here? I wondered. I was in a daze. Just put one foot in front of the other, I told myself.

I entered the emergency clinic and gave my name to the receptionist. Who am I really? I wondered.

"Have a seat; it shouldn't be long," she said.

What won't be long? I felt like asking. Maybe I'll get my hand fixed today, but what about my heart? How long will that take to heal, I wanted to inquire.

A few minutes later the nurse took me back to the examining room. I sat in silence for what seemed like an eternity. The room was white: both floors and ceiling. It felt like a cocoon. I waited, suspended in a surreal moment. Finally, I heard a faint knock on the door.

Before I could answer, the doctor poked his head through the door and entered. His white turban clued me in to his Sikh status. There was a large community of Sikhs outside Santa Fe. While I didn't know much about them, they could often be seen around town in the grocery store with their kids, on the Plaza, wearing white turbans.

Maybe he will be able to zap me with some healing energy, I thought to myself, half-seriously. The Sikhs were weird, some sort of cult, one more aspect of Santa Fe that made it unique.

"What happened here?" he asked quietly, turning my small hand over in his larger one.

"I slammed my fist on the table," I said sheepishly.

"You should have just let him have it in the face," he quipped.

Surprised, I started to laugh a little. The emotion quickly turned to tears, which I tried unsuccessfully to abate.

As he x-rayed my hand, I told him what had happened. He looked at me gravely, this mild-mannered man, and shook his head slowly. I calmed down.

"You won't need a cast. The fracture is so thin that it barely shows up on the film," he said. He told me to ice it off and on for the next couple of days if it started to swell.

As the doctor was leaving the room he turned around and looked at me deeply without saying anything for a full thirty seconds. Then he smiled slightly and went on his way. I gathered my things and checked out.

The look stayed with me. It was kind but piercing. I felt that he looked straight into my soul and saw how wounded and scared I was. His smile reassured me that perhaps there was hope for me after all.

I started to cry again as I got into my car and drove home. How would I live, where would I go, what was going to become of me? I wondered. But somewhere deep inside I, too, was relieved. The nightmare was over. My life could begin anew.

I spent the night alone in our bed, now just my bed. I knew he wasn't going to show up in the middle of the night.

The next day, through my tears, I moved all of Michael's belongings into the garage. Calmly, and with an inner conviction that was laser-focused, I called a locksmith and had the locks changed.

I called Michael at his friend's house, where I assumed

he would be staying. It was with another Belgian guy. Belgians had a way of finding each other all over the globe and, once connected, were best friends instantly. The guy's name was Geert. He, ironically enough, had been married to an American woman and had since divorced her. He owned a bakery in town.

"Hi. I'm looking for Michael," I said to Geert on the phone.

Dead silence.

"This is Sara," I clarified, not knowing whether or not there was, perhaps confusion with the other woman.

Geert cleared his throat. I could sense awkwardness on the other end of the line.

"Listen, Sara," Geert said at last. "Michael isn't here."

"Okay," I said deliberately. I sensed there was more to the story.

"Do you know where I can find him?" I asked. I figured Geert was covering for Michael and of course I did not want to go into any sort of an explanation about what was going on since I knew that Geert was well aware.

"Look," Geert said, "I can give you a number for him—for where he's staying—with Anne." My stomach reeled and a wave of nausea swept over me.

Anne. This woman had a name. After the nausea, it was anger that flushed through me. Before I had a chance to think I dialed the number. She answered.

"I need to speak to Michael," I commanded. She must have handed the phone to him immediately as I heard a very distant hello. The Michael I had known was simply gone.

When I heard his voice, I went ballistic.

"You need to come get your stuff today," I hissed. "I'm

moving everything into the garage and if it's not gone by garbage day, it's going out onto the curb for the garbage men to take."

"I can't believe how cold you're being right now," Michael said. He seemed shaky; close to tears. "I don't even recognize you."

I actually laughed then, unemotional, sarcastic, before another wave of hysteria washed over me and I was too overcome with grief to say anything else.

"Sara," I heard his muffled voice, soft for a moment and then when there was no response from me, harshness took over. "Yup, okay, I'll be out a' there. I'll call first so you can be out of the house when I come."

Michael was making sure there was nothing left between us. Not a shred of kindness remained. I was left with the sharp iciness of Michael's emotional distance that I had fought so hard against for so long. It overcame me like a giant moving glacier.

I looked around and took a mental note of our stuff. What was mine and what was Michael's, Just about everything, it turned out, was mine except for Michael's clothes, personal effects, and his tools, which were already in the garage. How handy, I thought.

Then I shuddered. Here I was, just twenty-nine years old and already on my way to becoming a divorcee. It was another reason for my parents to consider me a failure.

At long last I was completely empty. Utterly spent and defenseless, when Michael and I split up I was underemployed. So drained was I from the move to Santa Fe and the ensuing break up that I felt my former life unraveling slowly, leaving me desolate, alone and without resources either inner or outer to really understand what was happening.

While I had enough money for the next month's rent, I had exhausted my savings financing the move and was literally living from meager paycheck to meager paycheck. I needed a plan but didn't yet have one.

I sat down at the kitchen table, the very table that I had pounded my fist on so recently. I put my head in my hands and, while I did not cry, I sighed deeply. The house seemed wrong for me then. I knew I would not stay here after the divorce.

The space was ordinary, not charming and way too big. The rooms were square, and the outside was cookie-cutter bland. I need to find a place where my soul can feel light, I thought.

I was definitely in a dark place, darker than I had ever remembered being in before. The lyrics of a song or a saying from who knows where came to me then: It's always darkest before the dawn.

I hoped fervently that the saying was true. I asked myself if things could really get any worse and I honestly had to think that they couldn't. I hadn't planned for this. I hadn't seen it coming. I had somehow thought that I could control people and outcomes and mold situations to my whims.

I believed in true love and happily after and a whole bunch of other fallacies like things will always turn out okay. Where in the world did I get those notions?

I didn't know it at the time, but the darkness was actually dissipating incrementally. Just to understand that bad things sometimes do happen to good people was a huge shift in my thinking. It was the crack that allowed a teeny tiny bit of light to shine in.

Michael picked up his stuff from the garage when I wasn't home. Over the next couple of months, I arranged for a no fault, no contest divorce and he signed the papers, sending them back to me almost immediately.

My plan then emerged through necessity: I had to get more roommates to make ends meet. They came and went without names or faces, mostly young women who were passing through town, checking out the scene. One worked at the Santa Fe Opera, another at the local newspaper. Someone else had only a bicycle for transportation and insisted on parking it in my kitchen at night.

I was in a daze for a couple of months, looking for work and then quitting jobs that I did get because they weren't what I had thought they would be. From working as a bookkeeper for a home-based family business to taking a job downtown in a clothing store, nothing piqued my interest enough for me to stay for more than a couple of weeks.

Gradually, the fogginess inside my brain dissipated and I began to think a little more clearly.

Finally, I found steady employment as an office manager at a practice shared by a chiropractor and a naturopath. The office was located in a restored adobe ranch house. The doctors practiced healing modalities I had previously not heard of, such as homeopathic medicine, in addition to those I had only peripheral knowledge of but had never experienced firsthand, like herbalism and acupuncture.

When they had hired me, they told me that they had previously had a hard time keeping anyone in that position for very long but, for some reason, they decided that my energy just felt right to them, so they offered me the job.

Maybe my energy felt right because I was tremendously overqualified and just as equally underpaid, I thought to myself. Nevertheless, the practical part of me was thankful for the regular paycheck, small though it was.

I gave up the house and the roommates and moved into a tiny adobe duplex I found through an ad in the newspaper. I rented my half from the woman who owned it. Liza was an eccentric trust-funder who lived outside of Santa Fe on a spacious mesa. She called herself a Rebirther, which was something I had never heard of. But, in reality, she was a trust-funder who didn't need to work for money so spent a lot of time just hanging out.

I acquired a cat named Rex. Life settled into a new normal. I was functioning, some days well and other days not so much.

Nellie had been pretty much out of touch during my divorce. She had a way of fading in and out of my life. Now that I was free and single, Nellie was back.

I gave her a call one morning, just to chat.

"Hi. It's me," I said to her on the phone. "I'm calling you from my new home."

"Well, Sara," Nellie sighed, "I'm not one to lecture, but from where I'm sitting, this was inevitable. Just be thankful you got him out of your system."

"What'd ya mean?" I protested.

"You know all too well what I mean," Nellie commanded. "Be grateful you came through it okay."

"Yeah," I sighed. There was no use arguing with Nellie under any circumstances. But especially when I knew she was right.

Nellie moved on.

She began to talk to me then about an acupuncturist she had been seeing who worked with "energy," Nellie's word. Nellie was really excited about the work she had been doing with Anastasia, saying she was helping her clear her "karma" with her ex-husbands and release a lot of her "blockages."

"Sara, this is the perfect moment for you and Anastasia to meet," Nellie said.

In that instant, I couldn't agree more. Although I had a roof over my head and a mediocre income, I was barely hanging on emotionally. My heart ached all the time. I was lonely and lost.

DARE TO MOVE
THROUGH THE DARKNESS

Never fear to deliberately walk through dark places, for that is
how you reach the light on the other side.

~ Vernon Howard

"Here I go again," I said to myself as I drove down a
long driveway, lined with pinion trees and scrub oak. "On
my way to meeting another healer." But this time I was
prepared. After all, I had actually done some research
before meeting Anastasia, on acupuncture, and more
specifically, its use for inducing transcendental states.

Anastasia Morningstar (I doubt that was her real
name) came from a long line of money. I heard she had
disowned her Texas oil family, taken her inheritance, and
bought a Santa Fe style mansion to practice esoteric arts,
one of which was acupuncture.

And it was for this reason that I was proceeding to
Anastasia's place now. To receive the first of a series of ten
treatments, designed to open my third eye, the key to my
intuitive knowledge, she had told me earlier that week on
the telephone.

Third eye? What in the world was a third eye? I
wondered. And was it real? As the daughter of
psychologists, I had learned from an early age not to
believe in anything that couldn't be proven. Facts were

tangible, therefore real. The physical world was all that existed. There was no God, no Universal Intelligence that created the world, and no such thing as a third eye, part of the body's chakra system. According to rational thought, chakras, energy vortexes that lined the body, did not exist, except for in the minds of wackos.

In spite of my skepticism of all things New Age, I had begun to seek out information on my own. In the week that had passed between my setting the appointment with Anastasia and the visit on this day, I had read Shirley McLain's account of her acupuncture sessions with Chris Griscom in Santa Fe. Anastasia had studied with a similar group and was, she had told me on the phone, doing very similar 'work.'

This was pretty cool, in my mind; hanging out with someone who knew someone who knew Shirley McClain. Maybe I wasn't such a loser after all.

My thoughts were coming fast and furious. One minute I was thinking, yes, this is a good idea. The next, I was thinking I was a fool. My emotions ran hot and cold. No sooner did I justify my visit with Anastasia by likening myself to Shirley McClain when I became apprehensive.

As I faltered, I began to second-guess myself along with the entire strange inner journey I was undertaking. I hated needles, I reasoned, so, why was I voluntarily going somewhere to get them inserted into various points on my body?

However, right on the heels of the doubting thought, a small voice whispered inside my head. Go Ahead. Trust. And so I did. I knew that for some reason I was drawn to this healer. I figured I would find out why, and I hoped it was for a positive reason.

The drive from my home in the outskirts of town to Anastasia's house in the ritzy part of old Santa Fe was about thirty minutes. It was a sparklingly clear day with not a single cloud in the sky and I felt almost euphoric as I looked at the open vistas before me. I actually was getting used to the spaciousness of this place.

Then I entered the city limits and drove straight west to the foothills where actual mansions still existed. Nouveau riche meets old money. Hundred-year-old that houses that flaunted Spanish-style architecture existed next door to modern-day Santa Fe style adobe "castles" with skylights.

I located Anastasia's address and, sure enough, her place fell into the modern category. I parked in front of her house and walked to the door, beginning to feel strange all over again.

I placed my hand upon a brass knocker shaped like a dolphin and knocked three times. Hard. Anastasia came to the door wearing a cotton turquoise tunic and matching turquoise leggings. Her gray/blond hair was long and tied up in several elaborate knots. She wore a crystal pendant around her neck, a long, elaborate rose quartz highlighted with semi-precious stones: moonstone, amethyst, and aquamarine. It shimmered as the tip of the quartz dipped gently beneath her V-neck.

"Hello," she said, smiling warmly.

"Uh... Hi," I said.

Looking down at my faded jeans, worn black t-shirt, and flip-flops, I felt suddenly underdressed and outclassed. Who exactly was this radiant creature?

Anastasia's smile was warmly reassuring, however, and as I smiled back at last, she showed me into her studio, as she called it, an oblong room with windows lining one wall. Sunshine poured in, filling the room with golden warmth.

Books lined the other wall. I silently cataloged various titles in my head: The Seth Books, astrology, Chinese acupuncture and herbs, meditation, Tibetan Buddhism, soul mates and spirit guides. At the far end of the room was a table with acupuncture equipment, crystals, moxibustion herbs, candles, and various other unfamiliar-looking trinkets.

"Go ahead and have a seat for a minute," Anastasia said as she motioned me to a small chair by her massage table. She sat near me on a similar seat.

"I am going to have you fill out a brief questionnaire on your medical history," she told me. "Then we will talk a bit about my work before we begin the session."

A bit too eagerly, I took the form attached to a clipboard and began filling in my name, address, date of birth, etc. I wanted to get the preliminary stuff over with so I could abate the fear related to needles that was creeping up my spine.

While I filled out the questionnaire, Anastasia busied herself by taking packaged needles out of a cabinet and placing them on a flat plate. As she worked, she provided short explanations.

"I use only sterilized ultra-thin needles," she said. This was actually not very reassuring to me at that moment.

Is it too late to reschedule? I wondered.

"I studied at the East West College here in Santa Fe," Anastasia continued. "I am State-licensed to practice acupuncture here in New Mexico."

"Did you learn how to do past-life regressions there

too?" I asked, as my interest was piqued.

"No, I received a certificate from the Deva Foundation in Cerrillos, New Mexico, to practice esoteric acupuncture. My credentials are all here," she said, pointing to the wall behind her.

"Wow," I said, as I looked with genuine interest at her many diplomas from institutions both mainstream and alternative hanging on the wall.

She then pointed to the massage table and said, "In a moment you will lie down here on the table and I will begin to insert the needles into various points on the meridians, which is the English translation for Chinese energy pathways that run along both sides of the body and correspond to various organs."

"You will remain fully clothed during the session," Anastasia said matter-of-factly.

Whew, I thought. That's one question I don't have to ask.

"Any questions?" Anastasia asked, right on cue.

"Will it hurt?" I blurted out.

She shook her head and her expression told me that she got that question a lot. "You will feel small tingles when I insert the needles and again when I take them out. Other than that, you will hardly be aware that the needles are there."

And so, fully clothed, I lay down on the massage table and let Anastasia insert needles into my body.

She began with my calves and feet and then proceeded to my forearms and hands. After feeling the first couple of needles go in quickly and neatly, I realized it was true what she said about very little pain being involved, and began to just relax and let it happen.

As I lay on the table, needles stuck into my hands, wrists, feet, ankles, temples and scalp, I felt very vulnerable. Anastasia had total control. But, the needles themselves were going to work then, and because of the exactitude of the points on the meridian that she was focusing on, I began to drift off into a dreamlike sleep before Anastasia pulled me back from the brink.

"Describe to me what you are seeing," she commanded.

I obeyed, sensing the futility of arguing with someone whom I had trusted to render me utterly helpless. As I lay on the table like a porcupine, Anastasia definitely had the upper hand. At first, I saw nothing, only shadows, but at Anastasia's gentle prodding the shapes began to take on form and color. Suddenly a vivid memory began to play itself out with real-life intensity in my mind's eye.

"Watch out for the mailboxes," Robin screams, but it is too late. While driving, I plow right over them and straight into a tree. The next thing I know, there are sirens surrounding me and police cars everywhere. They are asking me to blow into a bag. If I refuse, I am automatically guilty. If I do not refuse, they will find out I have been drinking.

Another image flashes through: me sitting in my parents' living room. My mom is screaming at me because I have wrecked the family station wagon after getting drunk and passing out at the wheel. It is the middle of the night.

"You stink," she yells abruptly, in a high-pitched voice that hurts my ears. She keeps screaming. She is hysterical. How can my younger sister and brother remain sleeping through all this?

I believe she is referring to the way my breath smells, not that I stink as a person. Still stunned, though no longer drunk, my thoughts swim in circles in the too-bright room.

Where am I? Okay, I am lying on a massage table with acupuncture needles sticking out of me. But, the emotions from the past had seemed so vivid just a moment before.

"Sara, what we are doing together now is clearing that dense negativity from your past," Anastasia drawled. I hadn't noticed her southern accent earlier. I had forgotten the room, the table, the sunshine floating in all around me, the needles which began to itch and burn slightly as she removed them nimbly. She was standing beside the massage table and looking down at me. "As you remember scenes from the past, I am visualizing the darkness releasing into the light."

I was in no shape to question. I had the realization then that the impact of my childhood upon my life's choices stretched onward, far into my early adulthood, as I struggled to grapple with an inner pain that seemed to have no end. "It only appears endless," Anastasia drawled softly.

On the outside mine was an average family. But as I rode my bicycle around the smooth, rectangular neighborhood sidewalks, I felt numb most of the time. I had felt this familiar numbness overtake me as my mother berated me with every bone in her body that night I wrecked the car. She had come too far and suffered too long to end up like this, she said, referring to the spectacle of me in my broken down, disheveled state.

"Your pain is your beacon. It will illuminate your true self to you if you trust it and follow it—believe it or not, there is a path through the darkness that is yours and yours alone and if you dare to walk that path, your life will be forever transformed from one that honors fear to one that honors love," Anastasia said gently.

The acupuncture session ended. Anastasia left the room for a few minutes while I got up off the table, slipped on my flip-flops, and gingerly rubbed the tops of my feet where some needles had recently been removed. I combed my hair and smoothed my tee-shirt over my jeans. I was feeling relieved that I had made it through the session but also very disoriented.

When Anastasia came back, I frantically tried to ask questions, but she just smiled, handed me an appointment card for the following week and told me to go home and relax, not to strain myself for several hours and to drink a lot of water. It will detoxify you, she said.

Five minutes later, I was walking down the pinion-lined path toward my car. It was late; three hours had passed. I didn't understand what had happened in there.

I opened the car door and sat down in the front seat but did not start the car. I took a long slow drink from my water bottle.

Although I had just turned sixteen at the time of the car accident, my friend Robin, her boyfriend Jack, and I had been carousing at the college bars. I had just gotten my driver's license.

Robin was about to leave the country for three months of study in Ireland. This was her good-bye celebration. The Bon Vue Inn, a swanky bar and pool hall overlooking the ocean, was our chosen destination. Unused to drinking, and feeling strangely adventurous, I sampled various shots, wines, and brands of beer that night, not having been informed that it was unwise to mix liquors. The fact that three high school kids were allowed inside was odd, especially on a weekday. But we lived in a college town and could pass for co-eds.

Kingston, Rhode Island, home of the state university, sits on the edge of the north-Atlantic seaboard. While summers are picture perfect and the rocky beaches a playground for ocean frolic, New England winters are dreary, bone-chillingly cold and often foggy, due to the proximity to the sea. It was on an early spring night on Ocean Road, a dimly lit curving stretch of asphalt, where I passed out at the wheel and crashed the family station wagon into a tree.

The minute cops pulled up, Jack disappeared into the shadows, leaving only his head print in the front windshield. A lone strand of black hair wafted from a thin crack in the glass. If I had been going a little faster, Jack's head would have gone through the windshield.

"We're taking you to the station until we can notify your parents," the cops told Robin and me.

The cops brought us to the station and put us in a holding tank, a small cell with bars. I was furious. How could this be happening to me? Cornered, but not defeated, Robin and I screamed obscenities at the cops from our makeshift cell.

"You guys are nothing but a couple pigs," we yelled into the night. Looking at each other for encouragement, we laughed uproariously and shouted out a couple more swear words just because we liked the way they sounded. The lethal combination of booze and puberty fueled our rebellious and fanatical tirade until our fathers arrived to take us home.

My father looked weary, in his worn bell-bottomed jeans and tan sneakers. He had thrown a gray hooded sweatshirt over a white tee-shirt, which he'd likely been sleeping in. A faded green baseball cap concealed his almost completely bald head.

My father averted his eyes as he sternly grabbed me by the elbow and ushered me into the car, borrowed from the neighbors in the middle of the night. I imagined him making the dreaded phone call, waking them up to the terrible news: his darling princess in a car accident, intoxicated, in jail. Defeated, my father's failure was more acute than my own, as the horror of what had happened filled the space between us in the front seat with a tense silence. The shame seeping from his every pore was almost palpable.

"For an honor student, you're pretty dumb," he said a little too loudly as we settled. I slithered down in the passenger seat, wanting to bolt. I said nothing the entire way home.

My father was a college professor, head of his department and pillar of the community. With his rural Pennsylvania roots, he was the only child of a coal miner who had to eat jelly sandwiches for dinner during the Depression. My father had risen up to give me a better life.

My parents had met in graduate school. My mother was the Brooklyn-born daughter of East-European Jewish immigrants. Her mother, my grandmother, arrived on the shores of Ellis Island at age fourteen, alone and terrified, and never learned to read or write English.

My mother married young the first time around, running off to California with a soldier and earning a college education alongside her husband. She married my dad two years after her first marriage ended. Together they had three children, all born two and a half years apart, of which I was the oldest. My parents moved their fledgling family to Kingston, Rhode Island, where both were professors at the University of Rhode Island.

After an interminably long drive, my mother too had her say. When we pulled into the driveway, my mother's short, stocky frame was outlined in the doorway. I ducked inside, trying to bypass her, feeling like a whimpering puppy. Once in the house, however, there was nowhere to run.

My mom turned on all the lights downstairs. Although it was four a.m., it looked like high noon inside. It was a chilly evening and she wore a heavy green robe over her baggy pajamas and tan house slippers. She ushered me into the living room, where generally only formal dinners occurred. The faces from their mask collection glared down upon me as I sat in dazed distress. Every inch of wall space in my parent's living room was covered with souvenirs from their trips around the world and paintings and other artworks done mainly by their many talented and exciting group of friends. I longed for a simple empty corner on which to rest my gaze.

My mom sat down across from me and my father stood off to the side, looking concerned. I sat for a few moments, writhing under her glare and their unexpected attention. Usually I had a lot more wiggle room.

When my parents were through with me, I fell into a sweat-soaked bed, tears silently streaking my face. All I wanted then was to be left alone. If I couldn't die right then and there, on the spot, then I wanted to become invisible.

Somehow, I survived the night. The next morning,

Mom and I drove to the police lot to survey the damage done to the car, my eleven-year-old brother Josh in tow.

We got out of the car and surveyed the damage. The fact that none of us was injured during the crash was incredible when viewed against the backdrop of the demolished automobile. The front seat, where the three of us were riding, was smashed all the way into the back seat. The car was knocked completely askew, lifted off its frame, and totaled, according to police.

"Take a good look at what your sister has done," my mother remarked incredulously to my little brother. His eyes, the size of Frisbees, were glossed over with tears.

I stood in the parking lot, my hands in my jacket pockets, my brain foggy and uncomprehending.

Shit, I thought, I could have killed someone. Not only that, I actually could have died.

The numbness was wearing off and replacing it was a horrible reality.

"Let's go," My mom said. And we went home. My parents never spoke to me about the incident again. They bought a new station wagon, took me to court, and observed solemnly as the judge revoked my driver's license for six months. Many years later a therapist I was seeing told me the whole thing had very likely been a masked suicide attempt on my part.

When we were adults, Josh told me that when he got old enough to get his driver's permit my mother warned him, "If you drive drunk, there's either going to be a murder (yours), or a suicide (mine)." This directive came on the heels of my sister's drunk driving arrest, several years after mine, during her freshman year of college.

My brother, the youngest, turned sixteen after my

mother's patience in this area had been pushed to the breaking point. But this was the best she could do at communicating her feelings.

Still in my car in Anastasia's driveway, I felt drained emotionally, yet grounded in a way I could not ever remember feeling before. I realized the sun was setting. I rolled down the window and took a deep breath of pure-smelling air. The evening felt soft and warm like a cotton wrap caressing my bare shoulders.

Reaching down into my psyche to touch those painful memories from my past provided me with a huge sense of relief. A wave of quiet peace washed over me. My past was right where it belonged: in the past.

Just as quickly, the peaceful feeling vanished, and I felt sad and alone. The bewilderment was so profound that I heeded Anastasia's advice when I got home, falling into bed and wondering what the next day, and the next part of my life would bring.

AS THE CROW FLIES

The conscience can be a strong guide in life if we allow it.

~ Joyce Meyer

The next morning, I drove up to Hyde Park Wilderness Area and left my car at the base of the Santa Fe National Forest in the ski area parking lot where several trailheads leading into the high country converge.

It was Saturday. I had the whole weekend in front of me to get grounded from the acupuncture session the day before, and to clear my head.

I was in the midst of a deep healing process from the divorce and my feelings were often raw throughout the days for no apparent reason.

I started on the first trail that was nearest to my car. After hiking a bit, I noticed a steep trail going straight up and I set out upon it.

The mountains just north of Santa Fe are deep green and friendly. They jut upward from dry flat land, alive with rushing creeks and aspen groves amid brown, craggy peaks.

As I climbed steadily, my breath froze in my throat, but still I pushed onward, wheezing, gasping, and waiting to break into an even stride. Waiting for the relief and the release that came finally when, heart pounding in my temples, I felt like I could hike forever.

In moments like those, I found I could lose myself in the space around me. No thoughts or feelings would penetrate my awareness. It was this Zen moment I craved and was able to temporarily achieve on the hike that brought blessed relief. For me, hiking was an ideal way to let go of worry and just be. I experienced it as a kind of moving meditation.

I walked, not thinking, just sensing, letting images and impressions flow in and out of my awareness as my mind stretched out to meet the sky, and my coiled emotions unwound into the vastness of the land.

After about fifteen minutes, a lone black crow began to circle above me, crying incessantly. I looked up, distracted at first, lost in space and time. But the crow came closer, swooped downward and almost brushed my shoulder before settling into a nearby tree, still squawking.

I took notice then. She was large, her feathers so black they shone iridescent. Was she watching me? Yes. Was she trying to get my attention and somehow communicate with me? Impossible, my rational mind told me.

Since I was hiking alone, I looked for a marked trail or a landmark that would be so obvious that I could never in a million years miss it on the way down. I didn't have a great sense of direction so, as long as I stuck to the trail and carefully cataloged landmarks that were easy to remember, I figured I was good to go.

So, when I came upon an old logging trail that headed even higher, I decided to follow it. Turning onto the wide path, I ascended into a steep valley where shaggy, dark brown rock formations rose on either side of me.

Strangely, the crow followed me. Every time I checked,

she was flying just above me, circling in the ever-widening space between two peaks that lay ahead, as if urging me forward.

I hiked up a narrow ravine, setting my sights on a slick gray ridge of rock to my left. I walked, watching the ridgeline and I forced my lungs to take in more air than they knew how, simply to stop myself from thinking. I was trying to drown my thoughts in air.

The vivid memories that were stirred up during the esoteric acupuncture session the day before had left me unnerved. I felt unhinged, disconnected, spacey. Every feeling seemed magnified and out of proportion to what was really going on.

Before I knew it, I was high above the spot where I had left my car thirty minutes earlier. I looked down at the asphalt far below me and then turned my gaze to the faintly defined path ahead, leading further up a narrow crevasse deep into the Santa Fe National Forest.

I checked my backpack; it looked like I had enough water for a couple of hours of hiking. But the sun was oppressive and I would need to find some shade.

I decided to continue along this trail to the top of the ridge and go for the maximum view of the city of Santa Fe and the outstretched valley below before retreating via the shadowed side of the trail. The crow kept pace with me the whole time.

Once my agenda for the day was clear to me, I hiked with less fervor. Stopping to sip water, nibble on trail mix, look around, and breathe deeply. Eventually, the trail steepened; my pace slowed. I was nearing the top. When I looked up, the crow was flying miles above me, dancing in the sky. I imagined her saying, "Hey, isn't it gorgeous up here?"

Since I was pretending that she was communicating with me in the way that shamans have animal guides, I decided to try an experiment and communicate back. Telepathically I asked her what she wanted. In my mind, she replied, "Follow me."

So, I did. I reached the top of the cliff and saw the crow fly toward a pine tree dangerously near the ledge. I looked down and saw a large rock outcropping just below her.

I scrambled, trying to reach the spot where I could both sit and rest and also check out the view. I could feel sweat dripping down my forehead and my hair was damp underneath my pink baseball cap.

What if I actually fell while trying to maneuver myself onto that slab of granite jutting out into space? I wondered. There I was miles from town, alone, and bemoaning the fact that I had neglected to mention to a single soul what my plans were for the day. In other words, no one even knew I was up here.

I was still in a precarious spot, even though I was trying like hell to get some ground underneath me, I thought.

Nevertheless, I felt a sense of accomplishment, albeit temporary. I had climbed to the top of the ridge and that was no small feat. If my life was in shambles below me, at least I had made some progress on my hike.

I hoisted myself ungracefully over the rock and sat down. I was immediately floored by the view. I could see all the way to Santa Fe and the arid desert beyond. I could see the Jemez peaks in the distance, muted purple against a hazy sky.

I didn't know if the crow actually brought me to that

particular spot or not. The trail I was on led right to it. I wasn't simply walking in a straight line as the crow flies. But I was following the trail and there was a lone crow circling around me as I hiked. Truth be told, she was actually good company that day, if nothing else.

The crow flew high above me, and then circled lower. She seemed to like the rock I was perched upon and was using my body below as the center of her large circle's circumference, flying around and around.

I sat still for a while with my eyes closed then slowly opened them. I felt powerful sitting up there, to have made it to the top. All my problems that I had been struggling with seemed insignificant when faced with this vista, which dwarfed me.

I wondered if the crow had come to me this day as a sort of a spiritual teacher. Being around Nellie, Martin, and then Anastasia, I was getting used to looking for signs in my environment. Anastasia believed that chance encounters with spiritual teachers were not mere coincidences but true synchronistic events that propelled us toward our destinies.

Could those spiritual teachers include those in animal form? After all, I had been drawn to Santa Fe for a reason. And, I was beginning to feel I had been divinely guided, since I had arrived, to meet certain people and to experience certain events.

I had learned that in certain Native American lore, crows are messenger birds, straddling the space between the earth world and the soul plane, bearing wisdom from beyond. I wasn't Native American, but had I been visited by a messenger bird?

I had recently been introduced to Jamie, a Native

American author who had invented the Animal Spirit Cards, a deck of divination cards that depicted animals. Each animal relayed a specific message to the one who pulled it.

In fact, Jamie had invited me to a women's sweat lodge, a Native American cleansing ritual, to be held the following week. Coincidence? Maybe, maybe not.

Being far away from everyone and everything that was familiar to me, including Michael, had opened up the space for my consciousness to expand. I had come to the realization that I was not alone in the universe. In spite of my atheist/agnostic upbringing, I had come to accept that there was something, call it God, call it Universal Intelligence, which existed both within and around me.

I had begun to sense that my life had a purpose, apart from mere survival, which was all about a unique contribution that I and I alone could make.

After resting for a while at the summit, I realized just how tired and energetically spent I was. I took a deep breath, fully expecting the silence that accompanies distancing oneself from the sounds of civilization. Instead, I was met with what sounded like high-pitched laughter. It was the crow circling boldly right above my head. I could almost feel her mocking me. Her raucous cackle was jarring.

What the hell, I thought, I have nothing to lose so, I continued my experiment in animal communication. I looked up at her and tried to let her know I was aware of her presence and attuned to her message, whatever it was.

I asked the crow, "What is your message for me?"

I heard two words: "Slow Down."

I laughed to myself. My normally active imagination

was working overtime, likely fueled by dehydration, heat, and reading too many books on psychic phenomena and alternative healing that seemed to jump out at me from every library and bookstore since moving to Santa Fe.

Regardless, the crow, seemingly after having delivered her message, was gone.

I remained on the ledge and thought about what the crow had said. The message was spot on. Since leaving the East Coast ten years earlier, I had been wanting to slow down. The rush to acquire possessions and money had never made sense to me. Even as a child. I wanted something more, something deeper, from life. While growing up, I had often asked myself, "Is this all there is?"

I was always trying to read between the lines, dwelling in the gray area in a seemingly black and white reality.

Yesterday's acupuncture session had heightened that feeling. So many memories were dislodged during the hour and a half that I lay on Anastasia's table with needles stuck in me.

I was beginning to realize that my deep-seated desperation about being with Michael was not healthy. I was digging within my psyche for answers as to why I had placed him in such high esteem when he had treated me so badly for so long. It was three months since our breakup, and I was still searching for answers.

I didn't really date until I reached college in 1978. I was a timid, quiet teenager who lacked self-esteem. By the time I had met Michael, eight years later, I had dated a lot of guys. I had been in love and lust and been on the receiving end of love and lust. But, no one had gotten to me the way Michael had, and I was still trying to figure out why. To lose him still seemed like the worst thing that could ever have happened to me, even though a large part of me knew he hadn't been good for me.

The loss of Michael had left a vacuum in my life. I had no choice but to try to fill that emptiness with self-love. I was too flattened to even think of dating someone else or of leaving Santa Fe. This was the end of the road for me and, broke and broken, I decided either consciously or not, to stay put and wait until I felt either better, inspired, or both before deciding what to do next. I was stuck. I had no plan. And I was determined to wait for clarity before making a move.

So, Santa Fe was it, for the time being, for however long it would take. At that moment, this fact was just okay. It felt to me like I was, finally, beginning to make a spiritual connection, however tenuous.

Why here, and not anyplace else? Was it because of the region's history and earlier peoples?

I couldn't see them from the mountain, but I knew that there were nine Indian Pueblos forming a 150-mile ring around the city of Santa Fe, the only Pueblos in the country that were not eventually usurped by White settlers.

Indian life has continued uninterrupted in these Pueblos for a thousand years into the present day. In fact, Nellie had told me that ceremonial dances take place throughout the year that are open to the public.

Apparently, based on some local history I was beginning to absorb, when the Spanish settlers arrived in northern New Mexico four hundred years ago they erected rustic adobe churches on the pueblos. Spanish and Indian religion, food, and architecture eventually blended into a cultural mélange. I imagined drumming and loud, rhythmic singing echoing faintly throughout the spacious valley. The local Indians' indelible imprint of song and spirit wafted gently through the landscape.

After my rest, reflection, and summit view, it seemed like time to head down the hill. I gathered my strength for the trek down, repacking my backpack with my half-eaten lunch and power bar wrappers, and checking my water supply. Still one untouched bottle left. I eased myself off the rock and began to walk gingerly down the mountain as the afternoon sun waned.

Before I had gone very far, the sound of footsteps crashing through underbrush behind me startled me. A smiling, middle-aged Hispanic man came towards me. He was simply dressed in jeans and worn hiking boots and wearing a tan hooded sweatshirt that was unzipped partway down his chest to reveal a white tee shirt underneath. He wore a floppy felt hat and plastic dime-store sunglasses.

Obviously enjoying the same view of the valley that had so captivated me, he took a deep breath and casually said hello.

"Hi," I said, still somewhat taken aback by his sudden presence.

"Mighty pretty up here," he said gruffly.

"It is," I responded.

To my surprise, I wasn't the least bit threatened by this man who had appeared seemingly out of nowhere to disrupt my solitude. In fact, I welcomed his jovial unassuming presence.

"How much farther were you planning to go?" he asked.

My cheeks flushed. Not wanting to seem like the lightweight that I was, knowing that I was already on my way down, I said, "Maybe just a bit little farther. How about you?"

"I am headed up that way," he gestured toward the next ridge. "Would you care to hike along with me?"

"Sure," I said, surprising myself. I had just broken my cardinal rule of hiking alone, which was never to hike with strangers.

Accepting his offer, I began to hike with him much farther up into the canyon than I had planned to go or would have dared go had I been alone. We hiked through a high-altitude aspen grove filled with delicate new growth.

"This forest is stunningly beautiful," I remarked to my new friend.

"Yes," he replied. "There is a precise balance of elements on this planet, which is apparent in the awesome delicacy of the natural world. Plants, animals, rocks, water, all are intricately connected; all are a part of an interwoven web of life."

I wondered then who he was and why I wasn't frightened of him and why we were having an out-of-the-ordinary philosophical conversation deep in the heart of the Santa Fe National Forest.

We hiked on and the sun went behind a cloud and I realized I had no idea where we were, and I was disoriented. I was depending on him. Suddenly I began to panic. Had I lost my mind? Our hike had taken us to the top of one peak and into a valley adjacent to the one I had been climbing up earlier in the day. Would I be able to find my way down alone? I didn't think so.

I stopped to get my bearings, while he kept walking. After he'd gone several paces ahead of me, he realized I wasn't keeping up with him and turned to look at me.

"Are you all right?" he asked.

"I am thinking I will need to be turning around soon," I said hesitantly.

The stranger looked at me, clearly saddened. We made eye contact. And I sensed he meant me no harm. He was not in any way menacing or threatening. There was nothing whatsoever present in his vibe that signaled foul play. He seemed transparent, totally vulnerable, and unlike anyone I had ever met before.

My statement still hanging in the air, I let him lead me into a dark, dense forest where the sunlight, now slanting toward dusk, filtered thickly between large round tree trunks. Moss hung on the ground softening our footsteps and muting the sound of our voices.

"Do you think there is life on other planets?" my friend asked me.

I stopped in my tracks, my blood draining from my head, making it swirl. He seemed pretty different. It was almost like he was an alien himself. I was astonished.

"I'm not sure," I hedged. "Do you?"

"I think that life forms exist on other planets, yes," he said smiling simply in the twilight. "I believe that there are beings living elsewhere in the cosmos, very similar to humans and made up of similar elements, yet they differ slightly due to evolutionary factors."

I nodded.

"There are many beings from elsewhere living among us, disguised as humans," he added.

This time he didn't say he thought it, or he believed it, he just stated it as fact.

He seemed afraid he would shock me, but an inner

signal must have clued him in that I was ready to hear whatever it was that he wanted to say.

The day was taking a strange turn: first, the encounter with the crow, and then the unusual appearance of a guy who wanted to talk to me about life on other planets. Weirder still was the fact that I was listening.

I sensed that he actually could be one of them, an alien benevolently walking among us Earth folks, trying to spread the message of love and tolerance, of open-mindedness, reminding us of the beauty and fragility of our home planet.

This ordinary Hispanic man in his fifties of stocky build with short stubble of beard was certainly not who I would normally have chosen as a hiking buddy, nor as a companion at all, really. But here we were, conversing about deep philosophical questions, without even a proper introduction. I never even got his name.

From my vantage point in the wilderness that day, I realized that I could choose to believe whatever I wanted to believe. Whether it be the existence of animal guides, the inherent healing power of crystals, the existence of past lives or life on other planets, on and on, ad infinitum, I could explore these phenomena at my leisure and make decisions based on what I had personally experienced, rather that what I had been conditioned to believe.

A feeling of lightness overtook me then. I grinned up at the sky and breathed in the freshness of the evening.

"I am not totally convinced one way or the other whether there could be life on other planets," I said. I remained noncommittal. But inwardly, I was open to the idea for probably the first time in my life, simply because of the conversation I was having.

The day had somehow gotten away from me. I felt like my life was moving mysteriously in a direction I had neither foreseen nor had the power to control. The light was fading and my water was long gone. The sun was close to disappearing behind the mountainside and the temperature had cooled significantly. A breeze blew and chilled my sweaty skin. I shivered slightly.

I had started out earlier that morning on an ordinary hike. What had transpired, instead, had turned into a journey in and of itself. My decision to grow spiritually and to be open to guidance, from whoever and wherever it came, had in fact likely led to the appearance of two guides that day: the crow and the alien.

I was reminded of the expression, "When the student is ready, the teacher appears." I was certainly more ready than I ever had been for something tangible to base my life on that was not rooted in romance or finance, the two big issues that people in my AA meetings had stressed were ongoing in one's life and often tripped us up.

My companion and I climbed down the ski area trails. Our hike had taken us around to the closed trails and we scrambled down the barren, rocky pathways skiers use during the winter. I wasn't afraid; I was liberated and full of the mystery and magic of life.

As the sun dipped orange below the mountains in front of us, I gazed at miniature stars peeping out of the cobalt sky. Whatever was happening to me, to my mind and my life was good, I decided then. The experiences I was having were stretching me, pulling me outward from myself, my past, my upbringing, my conditioning into a new awareness that felt open, free, and completely unknown.

Finally, we had made it down to the parking lot, where

earlier perhaps twenty-five or thirty cars had been parked. Because of the lateness of the hour, there were only two vehicles remaining. Everyone else had long since left the trails.

The strange, or could it have been coincidental, thing about this was, my friend's nondescript brown truck was parked right next to my car. I shivered but said nothing. Was it there this morning? I couldn't remember. How could it be true? But there were no words and no answer came to mind.

"It was nice meeting you," I said shyly holding out my hand.

He cocked his head slightly and looked at me briefly but penetratingly, as if to acknowledge our time together. Then he simply quietly said: "Goodbye."

We parted quickly, casually, and unceremoniously. I can't remember if I said much of anything at all—not thank you—not it was nice meeting you, just maybe mumbling a short, "See ya," before moving away from him.

I walked to my car, climbed in, turned on my headlights and started the engine. The sun had just set and it was getting darker by the second. I began to wind my way down the mountain, lost in thought. The headlights from his truck followed me down and then, abruptly, were gone.

Where had he gone? Had he simply just vanished into thin air?

I let it go. It was late. It had been a long day. I couldn't think any more about what had or hadn't happened and who he was or wasn't. It didn't really matter because, I reasoned, I was perfectly okay in that moment.

DETOX TIME

No one saves us but ourselves. No one can and no one may. We ourselves must walk the path.

~ Buddha

My life in Santa Fe had settled into somewhat of a routine. I would go to work during the week and on the weekends, I would take advantage of all the City Different had to offer in support of my "spiritual quest," otherwise known as trying to "find myself."

At this juncture, I had been living in Santa Fe more than two years and I had come to realize a couple of things about spirituality:

1. There are many paths to spiritual growth
2. There is really only one destination—spiritual connectedness
3. No one can determine for me what my path should be
4. I have the opportunity to seek, find and live my own truth
5. As I am exploring, I can suspend judgment, and just be present with the experience

Once I got to this point, I started to have a little more fun. The seriousness of it all began to dissipate and I found I could even laugh at myself once in a while. According to

Nellie, this was a very good sign. I remember her telling me that the most spiritual people she knew of were also the most joyful.

A very serious dilemma remained, however. I was still searching for my particular path. True, there are many paths. True, there is one destination. But with so many spiritual options available to me, in the smorgasbord that was Santa Fe how was I to find the unique philosophy or religion, which would be mine?

Speaking of religion, in theory, I was raised Jewish. I had a Jewish mother, which meant, according to Jewish tradition, that I too was Jewish. But, while we celebrated the Jewish holidays with my mom's extended family in New York, we always celebrated Christmas and even had Easter dinner with my dad's parents in Pennsylvania, who were Methodist.

And so, I was confused from the get-go about religion and spirituality. There was never any discussion about God in my home growing up. My friend Wendy spent the night once when we were both about eight. We whispered to each other late at night, making sure there were no parents nearby to overhear.

"Sara, do you believe in God?" she dared to ask me. Her parents, like mine, were atheists, psychologists, and intellectuals.

"Um," I hesitated. "No, do you?"

There was a pause. "No," Wendy replied.

There was nothing more to say on the topic and we both fell asleep, knowing that we had done right by our parents in letting the God question go.

Both Wendy and me had Jewish mothers. Consequently, we were part of what my mom called "the

Jewish culture," not to be confused with the Jewish religion.

This was not easy to negotiate. In fact, it wasn't until my mid-30s when I took a Jewish History class in graduate school that I actually got this concept. The Jewish calendar, traditions and customs date back more than 5,000 years. The Jews were a tribe roaming the Middle Eastern desert, from whom I had descended.

Nonetheless, when kids would ask me what religion are you, I would always say Jewish. But inside I was saying to myself, but not really Jewish because my family didn't practice a religion and I didn't believe in God. Jewish was just something to say when asked the question.

This, like many paradoxes in life, turned out to be both a blessing and a curse. When was living in Santa Fe and engrossed in my spiritual seeking phase, the playing field was wide open. In spite of the obvious Catholic influences in Santa Fe, evident by the impressive and imposing Church of St. Francis right on the Plaza, I felt no more drawn to take a traditional approach than I did to something fringe or "new age-y."

What had made a lasting impression on me, however, from my childhood was the overriding sense that, should I choose to adopt a spiritual life someday, I would certainly have to pick one religion to practice wholeheartedly. Whether or not this conviction came from popular culture or was just something I had made up made little difference to me. I simply "knew" I had to follow one path and, by this time in my life, was wholeheartedly out to discover what that right one was.

While Nellie was still a large part of my life, there were times when she faded into the background. Nellie knew me better than just about anybody and always managed to keep tabs on me even if it was from a distance. I could and did call her often and share my experiences with her. For her part, I think Nellie lived vicariously through me. She loved hearing about my various adventures—experiences that were not available to her—as she was often struggling with money, barely managing to survive under the weight of raising three children on her own.

As my life unfolded, I began to make new friends, among those was a woman who had moved out west from Boston named Maureen—everyone called her "Mo."

Mo was a wiry woman in her mid-forties who had been an elementary school teacher. She had taken early retirement, sold everything she owned, and moved to Santa Fe to study acupuncture. (What else?)

Mo had never been married nor had any children, having lived a simple, quiet life. Though petite and mousy in appearance, Mo was actually a fireball. Once in Santa Fe, she was so intent on her spiritual search that it utterly consumed her day and night.

She took every seminar, participated in every workshop, and attended every book signing and psychic channeling she could cram in when she wasn't studying her acupuncture texts. As a result, Mo was in the know about all the happenings around town.

I had moved out of the house I shared with Michael and into an aging but functional duplex near the Plaza, the central downtown square that was blocked off to cars. The Plaza was a historic landmark, the traditional city center, where the huge St. Francis Cathedral sat amidst adobe-faced structures that housed modern-day shops and restaurants.

For all its quaintness and charm, the Plaza was more than just a tourist destination. It reminded me of being in another country, perhaps Mexico or Spain and of living in another time, maybe a hundred years ago, based on the architecture alone. Thus, the City Different nickname made more and more sense to me the longer I hung out here.

A couple years after my divorce, for all intents and purposes, it seemed like I was moving on with my life. However, the inner doubts that had plagued me upon my arrival still simmered beneath the surface.

Mo knew that getting divorced had made me feel like a failure at life and she was determined to help me snap out of it. Mo lived right next door and we often took walks around our neighborhood in the evenings.

We would walk downtown often and became buddies through our joint exploration of the shops, cafés, bookstores, and art galleries that contribute to Santa Fe's fascination.

One evening, we were walking around the Plaza after work and, in Mo's case, after class. I said to Mo, "Other people can get married and stay married, why couldn't I?"

Mo had no answer.

I, as it turned out, had a lot of answers but none of them satisfied me. I married the wrong person, I was too young, love is blind, he had affairs, etc.

"I should have known better," I told Mo. "Why the heck didn't I see it coming?"

Yet, when I had filed the divorce papers at the New Mexico State Courthouse in Santa Fe, I had hit a low that had caught me unaware.

"What a sorry end to the most passionate love story of my life," I lamented.

"The crumbling of your fragile world was actually a blessing in disguise," Mo countered.

I looked around me at the multitude of individuals, cultures, and classes that represented the local population. I had gotten used to seeing struggling street musicians, rich aging hippies, working-class Latinos, and extremely poor Native Americans all milling around the streets.

"Just think about all the soul-searching and personal growth this experience has led to," she said to me.

"I know, I know," I insisted. It was true. The end of my marriage had turned out to be the beginning of an amazing new chapter in my life, one I never in a million years could ever have anticipated.

The first time I'd met Mo, I welcomed her presence because I realized I wasn't the only one who was kooky enough to say I had been drawn to a place by mystical forces. It turned out I was not alone.

"You've gotten a lot more open-minded in the short amount of time that I've known you," she added. "You're a lot more fun than you used to be."

"I guess so," I said. It was true. I was actually starting to lighten up a bit.

We walked around for a little bit longer, then walked back to our neighborhood and said goodnight. When I got back into my house, I thought about what she had said. I realized that I was much more able to suspend judgment about spirituality and had come a long way toward being be able to be present with the new experiences I was having without having to analyze everything to death.

On one of our walks, Mo began to talk to me about a woman named Jamie, a Santa Fe resident and somewhat of a local hero, who had written several books. Jamie had recently become nationally known for her publication of the Animal Spirit Cards, which, as mentioned earlier, provide insight about animal spirit guides (of course!).

In my mind, I thought this was perfect timing. But I didn't mention my encounter with the crow to Mo. Some things were better left unsaid, I rationalized. Whether it was out of fear or being ridiculed or just wanting to keep the experience close to my own heart, I didn't tell her about it.

Occasionally, Jamie held Indian Sweat Lodge ceremonies on her land, providing instruction in the Lakota tradition, of which she was a part. Mo, as it turned out, had been invited to a Women's Sweat at Jamie's place the following week and, informed me that she would invite me along as her guest. Was it just my imagination or did these synchronistic events just keep falling into my lap?

I was up for it if Jamie was able to accommodate me, I told Mo. In truth, I was getting used to the out-of-the-blue meetings and experiences that were becoming commonplace in my Santa Fe existence. So, Mo agreed to ask Jamie about bringing me along the following week.

In the meantime, since it was Saturday and we had nowhere in particular to be, Mo suggested we stop into a coffee shop downtown. Mo was a self-professed coffee aficionado. We walked and talked while heading to our destination, the Lighthouse, a bookstore/coffee shop. Once inside, we made our way to a table. The Lighthouse was a beacon for spiritual literature and other stuff. Big bulletin boards towards the back of the store were cluttered with all manner of information on workshops, gatherings, art shows, etcetera. The coffee bar was upfront.

Once inside and seated cozily with our steaming mugs of coffee, Mo said, "Let's see if Jamie's book is here." Leaving our half-empty coffee cups on the table, we perused the book store's shelves, starting in the New Age and Spirituality Section, which was basically what the whole place specialized in.

"Here it is," I said as I found and pulled down the Animal Spirit Cards. It was actually a cardboard box that contained a set: the actual animal spirit cards themselves, modeled after traditional tarot cards. And then the book, which held detailed descriptions of the various animals depicted on the cards.

I immediately looked up the crow. The book said:

The meaning of the Raven symbol signifies that danger has passed and that good luck would follow. According to Native American legends and myths of some tribes the Raven played a part in their Creation myth. The Raven escaped from the darkness of the cosmos and became the bringer of light to the world. The Raven is associated with the Creation myth because it brought light where there was only darkness. The Raven is also believed to be a messenger of the spirit world. It is believed that Ravens who fly high toward the heavens take prayers from the people to the spirit world and, in turn, bring back messages from the spiritual realm. Other tribes looked upon the Raven as a trickster, or shapeshifter, because of its ability to adapt to different situations.

In general, Native American bird and animal symbols and totems are believed to represent the physical form of a spirit helper and guide.

I was stunned. There, in black and white was the answer to my encounter with the raven, in its form as a crow. I had found it in an actual book of all places. Tears came to my eyes right there in the aisle between two bookshelves as I read and reread the passage.

"Sara, are you all right over there?" Mo called from the counter. She had grabbed a copy of the book and was standing in line for a latte.

Her voice startled me. "Be right there," I answered in mock calm. I was still raw from the divorce and could descend into an emotional spiral at a moment's notice.

I can read more later, I thought as I tried to quickly pull myself together.

"My treat today," she said when I emerged from the back of the store, clutching the book for dear life and unsuccessfully hiding my red eyes. The pretense wasn't necessary though, as one look from Mo showed pure compassion. She understands and is okay with my sadness, I thought.

"Thanks," I said and retreated to our table to peruse the passage a bit more at my leisure. Darkness to light, messenger bird, the ability to adapt to varying situations... I knew deep within my psyche then that Spirit did exist. It was nameless, colorless, texture-less, and formless, but something made me pick up that book to validate my own, seemingly imaginary spiritual encounter with the raven.

Mo came back to the table with my latte and joined me in quiet contemplative reading. She was a true friend: not prying, allowing my space.

"This stuff is amazing," I said at last.

"I agree," Mo replied.

Before we left the store, both Mo and I had each purchased a copy for ourselves. By this time, I was totally hooked. I wanted to know more about Jamie and, upon hearing from Mo several days later that she could accommodate me at her sweat lodge, I was both anxious and excited to attend.

My anxiety stemmed from the fact that I was claustrophobic. Would I panic inside the sweat lodge or, worse yet, actually pass out? I tried not to think about either of those possibilities.

On the other hand, my excitement was genuine, as I contemplated the chance to experience something new and potentially life-changing.

I decided it would be good for me to seek solace from other women instead of looking for a man to fix me. I told myself I could really benefit at that moment by embracing the healing spirit of feminine maternal energies.

Mo and I set out for Jamie's land, where the women's sweat lodge was to occur. Jamie's house was about thirty miles outside of town and Mo was driving.

Everyone was instructed to bring a dish to share. After the sweat, there would be a feast. Mo had baked some sort of veggie casserole and I was simply bringing a loaf of French bread.

The sweat lodge was to begin in the early evening. But we left for the ceremony at around three to allow time to drive there, look around, and visit with the other women before "sweating."

As usual, the drive south of Santa Fe was gorgeous; purple vistas as far as the eye could see; pinion and scrub oak low to the ground, so dry the landscape could burn beneath the sun in an instant.

Mo and I were the first to arrive and I got a serious case of the jitters as we parked in Jamie's dirt driveway and walked up to the house. I wanted to talk to Jamie about her book, but Mo had cautioned me against it during the car ride there.

"She doesn't like to talk about it much." Mo had said. "She advised me on the phone to go get the book and read it before I asked her any questions."

When we knocked, Jamie came to greet us wearing jeans, a loosely fitting white cotton blouse, and sandals. A large woman with brown hair hanging past her bottom, she greeted us with a booming voice and a large smile. Her brown eyes gleamed with excitement.

"Hey, welcome," Jamie said.

"Jamie, what's up?" Mo replied as her tiny frame disappeared into the bear-like embrace of the much larger woman.

After they hugged, Mo motioned toward me and said, "Jamie, this is my friend, Sara, the woman I told you about."

"Great to have you here, Sara," she said. "You all ready to get hot?"

Before I could register this as a joke, she shook my hand, which, in similar fashion to Mo's hug, disappeared momentarily in her much larger one. I suddenly felt like a rag doll.

"Come on through and hang out in the back," she motioned. We walked into Jamie's house and then out the back door into her amazing yard that was more like her own campsite.

Picturesque and private, a small stream trickled through her backyard, winding and curving around the junipers and aspens that bordered the national forest just behind her land.

Jamie followed us.

As Mo and I milled around, about ten women arrived either solo or in small groups. Some I knew, some I didn't. With them came bread, salads, casseroles, teas and juices, fruit and desserts. Everyone placed their food on Jamie's large wood-block kitchen table and wandered around outside. Most, like me, had no idea what to expect.

"I started this fire a little after noon," Jamie told us, pointing to a huge fire burning in a fire pit on a grassy spot by the stream. "Underneath the burning wood are several dozen stones that are now absorbing heat for the lodge."

I looked at the blazing fire. Big round stones glowed like burning embers as flames dipped over and around them. In spite of the heat, I felt a chill run up my spine. What had I signed up for, I wondered silently. I looked for Mo but she was chatting with some new friends who had just arrived, happy as a clam and cool as a cucumber.

Next to the fire was a low round mound that resembled a canvas igloo: the sweat lodge. Jamie followed my gaze.

"I built this lodge last summer with a couple of friends out of green willows that bend around each other. We fastened a tarp over the top like a teepee and then added a pile of wool blankets over that to keep the heat in."

"Here is the door," she said motioning toward a flap at the front.

I didn't move.

"Go ahead and take a look, if you want," she said, reading the fear in my eyes. I leaned over and peered into the dark circular space. Blankets lined the dirt floor around a centrally located open pit.

The space was small and womb-like. I wondered how we would all fit in there. And if we would be touching each other as we sat inside like sardines. I pulled my head out and tried to stay present to what was going on. No sense in getting ahead of myself, I reasoned.

"We're gonna start the sweat at dusk and use the stones to heat the sweat lodge," Jamie explained to me and a few others who had gathered around. "I'll be pouring water over the rocks to create natural steam."

"I will serve as the 'door keeper'," Jamie continued. "Meaning I am the last one in and the first one out after each round. And I control the water and the heat." She grinned. "So that means you all gotta trust me with your lives."

Mo and I looked at each other with disbelief. Although she always appeared to be in the know regarding all this stuff, neither of us had ever been to a sweat before.

"Is this for real?" I whispered, more than a little paranoid at this point. Mo said nothing because Jamie was still addressing the group. She simply rolled her eyes slightly and shrugged.

"We'll do four rounds of sweating and then we should be about baked," she said.

Jamie went on to explain that she hosted sweats there regularly, usually once a month, on or around the full moon. This night was no exception. It was a Friday night in March, one day before the spring equinox and full moon.

I took a deep breath. Let's do this thing, I said to myself, realizing that I had come too far to back out now.

Besides, I could always bolt out the door if I couldn't take it, I reasoned. But that would be difficult considering Jamie was the doorkeeper and I would have to climb over her and whoever else was seated between the outside world and me.

As I stood outside, dusk settled and the moon rose, glowing pink in the deep turquoise sky. The afterglow was gorgeous. In New Mexico the sky stays light for a while after the sun goes down, illuminating the horizon in pale blue that fades very slowly into night.

We gathered around the fire that was now mostly coaling and Jamie began to shovel the glowing rocks out from under the burning embers and, pulling back the door to the sweat lodge, one by one she placed them into the once empty hollow in the center of the lodge.

We stripped, shivering in the cool darkness. To say that I felt weird was an understatement. Not only was I completely naked but also, I was outside and among strangers, in the company of all women.

I had always been fairly modest. I felt okay about my body but was not much of a sexy dresser. My style was sensible, practical, and comfortable. Although I was toned and fairly lean, I still felt ridiculously self-conscious.

Luckily, it was getting dark and all the rough edges—mine and everyone else's—were dissolving in the fading light.

One by one we crawled into the sweat lodge. We had to stoop low to crawl through the doorway. I sat down on the thick cushion of towels that lined the dirt floor.

Unfortunately, I found myself right in the middle of the circle, about equidistant from the door whether to my right or to my left. I felt completely vulnerable, sitting there, elbow-to-elbow with virtual strangers.

As we sat inside the lodge and shivered, Jamie, who was the only one still outside, began to load in the red-hot rocks. She shoveled them into the central pit and, as they piled up, the heat radiating from them was palpable.

As Jamie shoveled in the last rock, she entered the lodge herself with a huge bucket of water. Placing the bucket down beside her, she drew the door closed by pulling blankets over it and sat down by the door. She was the keeper of the door and no one was permitted to leave until we had done four rounds.

Soon the heat began to soothe me and, as Jamie sat down by the door and lowered the flap, I felt cradled in warmth, almost safe. Except for the coals, it was pitch black inside the sweat lodge. The blankets were so thickly placed on top of the lodge that no cracks of light (or air) could penetrate it.

Jamie began to talk more about the sweat process, explaining the rules as the ritual at last had begun in earnest.

She ladled water onto the rocks, creating steam that caused us all to gasp in the sudden intense damp heat. Again and again, she poured water onto the rocks until I felt I would suffocate. But I didn't. Instead, I began to sweat profusely.

Jamie passed around a stick she called a talking stick. As it went from person to person, we each spoke our fears out loud, releasing them into the steamy atmosphere.

This seemed appropriate to me. Not only was the cleansing process physical, but emotional and spiritual too. Jamie was using her Native American shaman gifts and training to call upon the elements to work in our favor.

"I want to move on from my divorce," I blurted out as I took the talking stick from the woman seated beside me.

"Ho," everybody else said.

The declaration seemed so finite to me. No sooner had the women sealed my words with their chant than I burst into tears.

It was a big sob that came forth, but no one seemed to notice as the talking stick was continuing around the circle and the steam was rising hot and thick in the tiny dark space.

During round one, I wondered how I would get through until the end. Gasping for breath and filled with panic, I thought of asking Jamie to let me out. But I sat still. Others too were having a hard time. One woman sobbed softly, another began to fidget, sighing loudly.

Then round one was over and Jamie opened the door, filling the lodge with cold fresh air.

"If anyone needs to, you can go outside between rounds," she said.

No one moved.

After about ten minutes, round two began. Jamie dropped sage onto the rocks and its sweet smell both comforted me and purified the space at the same time.

During the second and third rounds, the other women revealed more fears and shed more tears.

"I'm afraid my husband and I will never conceive a child," one woman said.

"I'm afraid I won't be able to get a decent job," said another.

"I fear always being alone," I said when it was my turn. I was moving into stream of consciousness where my ability to filter what I said was gone. I would have a thought and then would hear myself speak those same words, without completely meaning to reveal so much of my inner world.

At one point, my breathing felt heavy. I stayed put and tried to relax into the heat, as Jamie had suggested. Then it got easier as I gave up entirely, sweat pouring out of my body like a waterfall.

After each woman spoke the others would chant, "Ho," in unison. And between rounds, as the door was opened, we chanted a Native American prayer, "*Om mitaque asin*," meaning: all my relations.

As we began round four and the talking stick went from person to person, we were instructed to speak out loud what we wanted to manifest in our lives. True love, said one woman. A child said another. Freedom from despair, said a third. Money to build a house, said someone else.

"I want to love myself more," I said out loud. It felt so good to actually zero in on that concept.

In the unbearable cramped space of the sweat lodge, I felt very connected to the other women there. What each woman feared, I too feared. What each woman wished for, I too wished that for her.

As we sweated together in a circle and shared our pain and hopes with each other, the heat became somehow bearable until at last, the final round was completed.

"It's time to cool off now," Jamie said, opening the flap and climbing out.

We emerged, one by one, rosy and glowing. The ice-cold air felt like a slap into a new reality where everything glistened with a magical shimmer.

I felt light and buoyant, like I was suspended about a foot off the ground. I poured bucket after of bucket of tepid creek water over my head, letting the rushing chill hit me again and again, knocking me senseless with a feeling of abandon.

My self-consciousness was gone. I wrapped my hair in a big towel and pulled on my clothes. I was grateful for the layers I had brought along—underneath my parka were several big sweaters.

The others, too, seemed elated. We screamed and laughed in the moonlight like a bunch of coyotes. Wild women celebrating the night... celebrating life, I thought to myself. My inhibitions of earlier in the evening had vanished.

I began to feel myself being filled up with that Spirit; at first just a tiny trickle and gradually more and more good energy began to fill me with Love, seeping into my blood, organs, and bones, penetrating the tight, closed places within me like light pouring through an ever-widening crack in a door.

And, with that, the feast began. We ate and drank late into the night.

Mo and I were giddy on the ride home. We excitedly talked about the sweat.

"I couldn't believe how hot it got," Mo said.

"I know," I agreed. "I thought there was no way I would make it to the end, but it got bearable as I got used to it."

"That's what it felt like for me also," Mo said.

As we drove home, the headlights illuminating just a portion of the ghostly landscape around me, I was hit with a powerful insight: the experience of losing everything had put me in touch with what it was I could never lose because it wasn't mine to possess in the first place: Spirit. The essence of all that is, was, and will be, the truth of who I am. Vast, Magnificent, Unknowable.

When I got home, I collapsed into bed and slept soundly. It was a deep and dreamless sleep where my body just let go for a solid eight hours.

When I woke up the next morning, however, it was a different scenario altogether. I felt groggy and sluggish. It was Monday and I had to go to work. I knew I would be facing deadlines.

Because I was tired, everything and everyone I encountered during the day seemed to grate on my nerves. In spite of the fact that I worked for a small family-owned company, with only five of us on staff, I still didn't want to be around people.

"How was your weekend?" my boss Harv asked me as I arrived at the small office where book editing and layout took place.

"Okay," I said, sitting down at my desk and not volunteering anything else.

He gave me a sharp look but was kind enough not to pursue it and left me alone.

I felt moody and disconnected. As the day after the sweat lodge wore on, I realized I had completely lost my euphoria of the night before. Instead of high, I felt low; instead of exhilarated, I felt disappointed. What kind of an emotional rollercoaster was I on, I wondered?

SPIRAL JOURNEY

In the beginning, we may erroneously imagine spiritual practice to be a linear journey, traveling over a certain landscape to a faraway destination of enlightenment. But it is best described as a widening circle or spiral that opens our hearts and gradually infuses our consciousness to include all of life as a spiritual whole.

~ Jack Kornfield

After the glow of the sweat lodge experience wore off, I began to realize that my forays into alternative healing modalities were not going to cure me.

One step forward and two steps back was how I was beginning to think about my healing journey. Or, more realistically, I kept coming back to the same place over and over but had seemingly moved up a notch from where I was when I had first dealt with a particular inner obstacle.

I was making progress, but it wasn't linear. It occurred to me then that I was on a spiral journey.

For example, I was dealing with several issues, which I had made considerable headway in resolving. But they kept coming back in a new and slightly altered form.

One: Since my break-up with Michael, I had struggled with the concept of self-sufficiency. Feeling incredibly needy, I knew I had to heal alone before I could conceivably get involved romantically again. I tried hard to be brave and mentally let Michael go.

But day after day I was plagued by feelings of inadequacy and deep pain. I didn't sign up for this kind of life, I would tell myself as I went to work at the publishing company then went home to my apartment alone in the evenings. Life seemed sparse and barren, devoid of the fun and companionship that I envisioned would be mine in young adulthood.

Two: I struggled with loneliness. I often hiked solo on the Santa Fe trail, falling in love with the wide-open spaces and the lavender hues of the high mountain desert like they were my personal comforters in a time of feeling unconnected and lost. But it wasn't enough.

The people I met in Santa Fe were not like the people I knew growing up. Rugged, individualistic non-conformists populated the area, which offered a respite from the fast-paced, goal-oriented mentality of mainstream America. While many were interesting, and even fascinating, most didn't fit the mold I was used to so I often didn't feel an instant kinship with the folks I ran into in Santa Fe.

Then there was the ever-present question: Would I ever love again? I went out dancing on occasion and found solace in brief encounters with guys I would meet in the clubs. But I wasn't ready for anything deep so I kept my guard up.

My childhood friends were mostly married by this time. We had all hit thirty and kept on going. Many were becoming parents for the first time and progressing, as my mother would probably say, right on schedule. In other words, to use another of her favorite expressions, they were "settled."

I, on the other hand, was anything but. I longed for an

authentic connection with a man but was unsure about the settled stuff. Until I settled the unease within my own psyche, I really wasn't interested in the trappings of normalcy that would make my parents and my high school peers breathe a sigh of relief.

I remember Nellie telling me once, "Sara, it's an inside job. There's no point in building your life from the outside in. It just doesn't bring lasting happiness. Your life will unfold organically from the inside out and then what you create is really from your soul."

I actually agreed with her. But in the meantime, I had to find a way to live.

Three: In addition to personal struggles, I faced some real financial woes. In Santa Fe, there were few professional jobs. The economy was tourist and service-based, which made earning my living as a massage therapist a shoo-in. But I soon found out that if you didn't arrive in town with a trust fund in place, you were pretty much guaranteed some level of financial struggle just to make ends meet.

And struggle I did. I worked a variety of jobs, none of which was very satisfying or in any way connected to a "traditional career path."

I lived from paycheck to paycheck for the entire time I lived in Santa Fe. I was making barely more than minimum wage while at the chiropractor's office and mot much more than that at the magazine and the publishing company.

I was still driving the Toyota Corolla my parents had bought me ten years previously. A retirement account, or even a savings account for that matter, were naturally out of the question for me during the seven years I lived in

Santa Fe.

Thankfully, I always managed to pay my rent, utility bills and provide the basics for myself in terms of clothing and gas and car insurance. But I lived simply and without extravagance, which was actually okay once I got used to the idea that while I was choosing to be there, that was just the way it was going to be.

One day I decided to return to the Lighthouse, on my own this time. It was early fall and there was a little less intensity to the sun's heat as there had been just a few weeks earlier.

As I walked from my apartment to the Plaza, where the bookstore was located, I realized I had just passed the third anniversary of my move to Santa Fe. I was thirty-one. The streets and buildings as I observed them on my walk were familiar now. The ristras hanging outside tourist shops everywhere I turned didn't stand out to my vision anymore. Nor did it seem odd to see so many art galleries, crystal shops, or restaurants clustered together.

I belonged there, even if temporarily, I thought as I entered the Lighthouse and made my way toward the "New Age and Spirituality" section. I had wanted to look up spiral symbolism, since that concept kept playing itself over and over in my mind. It had appeared spontaneously, as if out of nowhere, and I couldn't stop thinking about it.

I perused the books on the shelves in no particular order, letting my eyes blur a bit as I made a mental plea for assistance from the powers that be. I discovered not one but many references to the Spiral in several different volumes that seemed to fall off the shelf right into my hands.

Much to my surprise, I learned that quite a few authors

had written about the spiral, including Carl Jung and Joseph Campbell.

What I found was something like this:

The spiral is the most widely recognized and repeated archetype used to symbolize our inner and outer journey to God and the Self. Spirals symbolically represent a passage into the collective unconscious and then back into the world renewed with a greater psychological understanding of who we are and why we are here. This journey provides what Jung called the transcendental function of the psyche by which we achieve what should be our highest goal: the full realization of the potential of our individual Self.

There was more:

Spirals symbolize our soul, our essence, remaining the same while experience deepens and elevates our egos, or personalities, simultaneously. The center of a spiral is the center of the Self as it goes through the forward movement of time, yet never loses the essential spirit of its origin. Ascending spirals represent the reconciliation of the old order (unconscious) with some element of new creation (conscious). The unfolding of the spiral is the soul incarnate unfolding upon itself time and again throughout our lives.

The fact that the image of the spiral to describe my inner journey had come to me spontaneously and completely independent of the words I was reading and the concepts they conveyed gave me goosebumps. To say that I felt validated was a complete understatement. Actually, I felt connected to others, throughout time, who had sought answers to deep-seated questions. Not only did I not feel foolish; I actually felt wise reading those words and realizing that I was having a universal experience.

I looked around me at the ordinariness of the bookstore: people browsing the shelves, seated in easy chairs, looking through books they may or may not decide to purchase. It was late September. The sun was less intense coming in through the double-glass doors than it might have been just a few short weeks earlier. Fall was coming.

In spite of my non-descript surroundings, I felt very fully alive in that moment. Everything around me seemed to vibrate with an invisible electrical current. It was thrilling.

It made me feel not so alone as I savored my discovery. Others throughout time had been seekers and, on some level, I felt very connected to them, although they were nameless, faceless and not present with me in space or time. I walked home in a cocoon of lightness and peace. The restaurants, shops, art galleries and ristras strung out to dry in front of many awnings were simply a backdrop now as I strolled oblivious to traffic and tourists alike.

It was a week or so after my experience at the Lighthouse that Mo and I decided to go with a new friend, Emmy, to visit some hot springs one sunny summer weekend.

Emmy was a transplant from upstate New York. She had bought some land outside of Santa Fe and, over the course of several years, at age thirty-five, had built herself a cabin, outhouse, and corral. Emmy had a couple horses.

She was blond and petite and could have been pretty if it weren't for her lined, leathery face that had become prematurely wrinkled from hours spent outdoors. She was muscular and didn't have an ounce of fat on her body. Her hair was long and eternally knotted. I wondered why she didn't pull it back but instead let it whip in the wind all day long, framing her tanned features like a mane.

Emmy kept in touch with the outside world by a battery-powered phone, which worked less than 50 percent of the time. Emmy could not care less. She made a living by taking nature photographs, making them into postcards and selling them to the local gift shops.

She had a beat-up old station wagon. We took her car on the trip since we would be driving through rugged terrain. Emmy swore by these hot springs. "They're good for whatever ails ya," she'd say. So, off the three of went to spend the weekend soaking.

Honestly, I was hoping for a fun break. Enough of the spiritual stuff for a bit, I was thinking. I just wanted to have some laughs with my friends.

As we drove north into the San Luis Valley, my heart softened at the beauty of the landscape before me: the road meandered through a dry, narrow valley walled on both sides by steep, rugged mountain ranges: the San Juans and the Sangre de Christos, Emmy informed me.

All that space rushed up to meet me in an instant as it knocked the very breath out of me. There had to be some sort of a higher power who had created all this.

I looked out into empty space. There were no trees or even vegetation to block the stark view of the horizon. Where was I, seemingly in the middle of nowhere?

New England, where I had spent the first eighteen years of my life, was wooded and dense with vegetation. The sky seemed smaller there and the horizon narrower.

The expanse of space made me feel agoraphobic. I also felt some fear as I realized my life had taken an unexpected turn. Here I was smack in the middle of unfamiliar territory with no clear direction one way or the other. I didn't want to go back to my old life. But I had no idea where I was going, literally or otherwise.

I turned on the radio, for a distraction, of course, only static. There was no reception in the isolated valley, and I doubted Emmy's million-year-old car even had a working radio in it. Too high-tech, I imagined.

"Where the heck are we?" I blurted out. "How far away from civilization are we planning on going here?"

In the backseat, Mo laughed. "Just you wait, Sara, you're not gonna believe this place we're headed. We'll be leaving the highway soon to turn onto a dirt road that goes straight up, over that way."

I turned to look. She motioned to her left, towards the face of a massive mountain peak.

"This is feeling creepy," I said. "We are really off the beaten path here. I am completely in the dark about which direction we're going."

"Some things need the darkness to take root," Mo told me; always bring things into the metaphysical.

I turned back around and looked out the window. I tried to believe her, and I tried to trust that which was unseen. I saw myself then as some sort of a control freak who wanted to know everything before it happened. And to always be able to pinpoint my exact location on a map. It gave me the illusion of security.

"You know guys, I don't really see where all this civilization has gotten us," Emmy said. "I mean I get along just fine without all the stuff most people spend their entire lives working for."

I pictured Emmy's outhouse and her primitive,

makeshift "kitchen" without running water. A big metal tank that collected rainwater was rigged up outside her kitchen window with a rubber hose that was somehow connected to an on-off valve that functioned as a faucet. If she wanted the water hot, she had to heat it on her wood-burning stove in a big, blackened kettle.

I thought of her weekly forays into the YMCA for hot showers. Emmy was really doing her own thing—in the true sense of the word—with not a single regret.

No thank you, I thought, but I admitted that she did have a point.

We were all quiet for a few minutes as the landscape we were driving through seemed to overtake our conversation.

In that silence, I began to ponder the concept then of faith—non-religious, non-denominational, pure unadulterated faith in a greater power that created the mountains, the sky, this awesome valley and even created me—not for some random, insignificant purpose but maybe to do something unique—to give something back during the short time I have allotted to me.

My thoughts were interrupted by a loud bang, followed by a bump and a jolt. We had hit a pothole and knocked the muffler off of Emmy's car. She got out, picked it up off the road, dusted it off a bit and hurled it into the back seat. The road was rutted and dry. Rocks were everywhere and I wondered about the condition of Emmy's tires. I forced myself to keep quiet.

The hot springs were high up on one of the mountain ranges. As Mo had said, there was a barely marked turn off onto a dirt road that wound around and around, in switchbacks as it climbed steadily upward.

Without its muffler, the car bounced loudly and uncomfortably along. All our camping gear rattled around inside the trunk. It was too noisy to talk. We rolled up the windows to keep the thick brown dust from the road from getting inside. But, true to form, Emmy's car had no air conditioning, so I had to continually wipe sweat out of my eyes with my sleeve.

Finally, parched and exhausted, we arrived at the aptly named Valley View Hot Springs, a large land-trust operated by a guardian, where a minimal admission price was charged for overnight stays. One could either camp in the onsite campground or stay in the lodge. The main draw, obviously, was the hot springs, which were healing and abundant. The entire place was deemed "clothing optional."

The land-trust, in an effort to keep the area's natural resources intact, allowed the building of only a few very basic structures. Far from quaint or cozy, the hot springs were rustic, minimalist, and actually about as natural as you could get.

As dusk was approaching, we wasted no time setting up our campsite. I set up my old reliable orange dome tent that I'd bought on sale from Sears years before. Unpretentious and plain, it did the job of keeping me sheltered from the elements perfectly.

As I unrolled my sleeping bag and foam pad, took out the various camping essentials from my pack: flashlight, extra pair of jeans, wool socks, long underwear, I felt a strange peace overtake and fill me. The place was so quiet and calming.

I stepped outside my tent and was immediately chilled. With evening in the high country came an instant but profound drop in temperature, as the thin atmosphere did not trap much heat after the sun went down.

Before me, the sun was setting over the most enormous valley I had ever seen, and I was on the edge of a vast expanse of emptiness.

The emptiness of the valley seemed less frightening to me than it had when we were driving. Maybe it was because I had arrived somewhere tangible.

Across the valley lay a pink and orange sea, more perfect than any paintbrush could ever duplicate. And then it was gone, disappearing into deep blue semi-darkness. "The only constant is change," I heard myself whisper then. "Nothing lasts. Everything transforms. Like life itself; like us. And in the middle of it all, it's just really beautiful."

Emmy poked her head out of her tent just then and said, "Hey, how about a soak before dinner?"

I was ready. We walked by flashlight up a small path and found ourselves at the first of a series of hot spring pools. "We'd better stick to the bottom pool for tonight," Emmy said.

So, alongside my friends, I undressed in the frigid night air and slipped into the warm soothing mineral water. There were other soakers around: couples, and families, about a dozen or so people of all ages relaxing, laughing, and sweating out their toxins here.

It reminded me of a scene from the '60s: nobody wearing clothes, everybody very mellow. But it was the healing water that was making them like that.

I took a deep breath and felt my muscles let go into the soothing hot water. It smelled a little like rotten eggs, which, according to Emmy was actually the mineral sulfur, which brought about muscle relaxation.

The communal bath out in nature was new to me and for a moment very scary. But, at the same time, it was freeing. I felt disconnected from the rigidity of my childhood I felt like my life was my own, realizing I didn't have to please anybody or follow anyone else's rules.

I was so far away from the judgments of my parents, teachers, and society in general that I laughed inwardly. All the crap I had been taught was so important, like fitting in and conforming to certain outward standards, just melted away into the hot mineral water.

The cool night enveloped me like a cape, letting my imagination soar. I could go anywhere and be anything I chose.

But then what would I do, I thought as I soaked. If I let everything go, would I die of starvation? Would I be able to take care of myself? Would I crawl into a cave and become celibate and meditate for the rest of my life? That notion, of course, seemed absurd.

I realized I did truly value work and relationships. Just a few more open-ended choices would be nice, I decided. And a little more time to feel things out for myself was also what I needed, I thought. I was taking that time and space now. It was blissful.

After the soak, the three of us climbed out of the water and dried off ourselves under the moonlight. We took the path down to the main cabin and cooked up some pasta, sauce and a big salad in the communal kitchen. The food tasted wholesome and satisfying.

I walked out of the lodge into utter darkness and peered up. The stars were magical and abundant. Being so far away from urban lights did have some advantages, I thought. I had never seen so many stars so clearly in my entire life. The sky was such a masterpiece that night.

Reluctantly turning on my flashlight, I followed the others back to out to the campsite.

The water had made me sleepy. The minerals had drained my muscles of lactic acid and my body ached for rest. Falling asleep to the sound of owls in the distance was somewhat eerie. Yet I felt safe in the nook of the mountain, cradled in the land.

The next morning, I was the first one up. A dizzying view greeted me as I emerged stiffly from my tent into the chilly air. It was late summer, but the high altitude and thin atmosphere did not provide much warmth as the sun was barely out. I looked at my watch: 7:30. The campground was perched on the side of a cliff that was not very sheltered by trees. Thus, the entire San Luis Valley lay before me. I felt small and cold.

I headed straight for the lodge kitchen to make myself a cup of coffee and to warm up. Unused to the starkness of the West, and certainly not familiar with remote camping, I was immediately fearful and needed to be indoors.

When I got back to the campsite, Mo and Emmy were chatting and getting their gear together for the day's hike. Emmy had told us that the best hot springs were about a half-mile away from the campsite and, she cautioned, straight up.

After a breakfast of apples, yogurt, and granola, we hiked higher than we had the evening before, following a well-worn path along a small stream to the top of the mountain where a series of three or four tiny pools lay perfect and pristine in a straight line equidistant from each other.

Each pool was a steaming opal, a deep, oval gem, inviting, enticing, and delicious.

I felt primitive, child-like, silly, and almost giddy as I removed my mud-caked hiking boots, wool socks, jeans, and layers: long underwear, turtleneck, sweatshirt, and parka. The sun was out finally, and, yes, it was warming up. In fact, it was turning into a beautiful, clear day with not a cloud in the sky.

I soaked, alongside my friends looking out over the wild, open, valley that seemed to swallow me up altogether, feeling as if suspended in outer space. My body seemed small and insignificant in the wilderness. I felt like I could lie down and die like an animal on the side of this cliff and slip back into the land, easily, effortlessly, falling asleep and merging with all that is.

Strangely, this thought didn't disturb me in the least. My anxious, over-analytical, always-thinking mind was still for a short period of time and, rather than feel upset about it, I was completely relieved. My problems were not monumental after all, when contrasted with so much space, distance, and height that had been afforded me by the landscape.

The day passed with great joy and adventure. I had been feeling so lonely since my divorce and had just wanted to go hang out with my girlfriends and take a break from all this hard, spiritual questing.

Ironically, in letting it all go, I started having some spiritual epiphanies like occasionally feeling connected to something greater than myself, all-powerful, all-knowing, and actually all-loving.

We spent another night in the lodge cooking and

hanging out with fellow soakers, then left the following morning. The drive home was fun, full of laughs and chatter.

Happily, I felt more connected to Mo and Emmy after our hot springs experience. We had bonded with each other over the weekend, having gotten closer from the being outdoors and camping together.

I started to worry again as we approached civilization. I had been living in Santa Fe for going on four years at this point and again was beginning to think about leaving...

Should I simply give up my spiritual questing at this point? If I did leave Santa Fe, could I somehow incorporate the fringe experiences I had had in Santa Fe, glean their lessons, and take them with me into the world at large? These were the questions that nagged me as I drove home from Emmy's land after our weekend at the hot springs.

The continuing and all too familiar question of whether or not to remain in Santa Fe weighed heavily on my mind as I bid farewell to my friends. While I enjoyed the company of Mo and Emmy, I was thinking about the friends I had grown up with and their orderly lives.

Mo and Emmy were East Coast transplants who were never going back. As for me, I wasn't so sure anymore where I was headed and, if I was going to stay in Santa Fe for now, how long would I live here and where would I go when my time there was up?

OLD MAN GLOOM

People have a hard time letting go of their suffering. Out of a fear of the unknown, they prefer suffering that is familiar.

~ Thich Nhat Hanh

As the years went on, my life in Santa Fe contained some constants: I kept my friendships with Nellie, Mo, and Emmy. I had certain routines that included hiking in the Santa Fe National Forest and walking around downtown. I cherished the familiar landmarks, art galleries, crystal shops, restaurants serving South-western cuisine, and tourist stores selling tee shirts and memorabilia.

The city, once so foreign to me, had actually become my home in the five years I had lived there. The familiarity felt good: streets, sky, grocery stores, mesas, various manmade and natural landmarks had become part of my everyday world.

What I could not get used to, however, was the constant hand-to-mouth existence I was living. I knew it would be close to impossible to ever truly get ahead since there was no industry in town except tourism. Even so, the longer I stayed in Santa Fe, the more comfortable I became.

Thus, a paradox was evident in my day-to-day reality. However much I might have wished that things were different, I knew with certainty that it wasn't going to be workable indefinitely to stay. Life was just too hard and uncertain.

There was constant pressure to earn just a little more money, as saving anything was out of the question. While I had moved to Santa Fe in my late twenties, I was by this time in my early thirties and my priorities had shifted. Gone was the constant search for new and exciting experiences. That quest was replaced, quite surprisingly, by a desire for roots and stability. However, I wasn't interested in moving back East where I had grown up. That much was also clear. I had left that life and was only interested in moving forward.

One of the reasons I liked Santa Fe so much and was loathed to leave was that I had found a community of not only spiritual seekers, but like-minded individuals who also believed it was okay to DIY spirituality. In fact, as I was soon to learn, Santa Fe had a precedent of merging various traditions and melding them into their own unique version.

On the weekend before Labor Day, Nellie invited me to attend the festival known as Zozobra with her and her kids, which I'd never been to. I was interested in doing something to mark the transition of seasons. While the days were still warm, in fact sometimes up to almost eighty by noon, the evenings were cool and the nights and early mornings were downright chilly. There was definitely change in the air.

I agreed to go and then promptly looked up Zozobra in a Santa Fe tourism flyer and here is what I learned:

Zozobra ("Old Man Gloom") is a giant marionette effigy that is built and burned every autumn during Fiestas de Santa Fe... As his name suggests, he embodies gloom;

by burning him, people destroy the worries and troubles of the previous year in the flames.

Well, why not? I thought. At that moment, I felt myself as being so much more open-minded than the me who had arrived in Santa Fe five years prior. Looking back, I saw myself as a scared, narrow-minded person who was clinging to a mere idea of a marriage with all her might. Knowing that the marriage had crumbled, based on hindsight, I could actually gauge progress in my psyche since those early days. My energy level had become much more robust. I had weathered so many storms in Santa Fe and, almost in spite of myself, had grown emotionally. I had morphed into a newer improved version of me as a result of hardship and inner searching.

So, let's see about letting go of a bit more doom and gloom, I decided.

The festival sounded like the perfect place to do so. I read in a tourist pamphlet that the Fiestas celebration began in 1712 to celebrate Don Diego de Vargas, who had conquered the territory of New Mexico. Zozobra had been incorporated into the Fiestas in 1926, and the Kiwanis club began sponsoring the burning in 1963 as its major fundraiser.

I also learned that local artist Will Shuster conceived and created Zozobra in 1924 for a party at his home for artists and writers in the Santa Fe community. His inspiration for Zozobra had actually come from a celebration of the Yaqui Indians of Mexico that incorporated the burning of a puppet. Shuster and friend Dana Johnson, a newspaper editor, had come up with the name Zozobra, which was defined as "anguish, anxiety, gloom," or in Spanish "the gloomy one."

Nellie told me that upwards of 30,000 people go to watch Zozobra every year and that the puppet actually stands fifty feet tall. The Kiwanis Club of Santa Fe builds Zozobra and burns the effigy annually at Fort Marcy Park.

Fort Marcy Park, actually a baseball field and home to several local kids' baseball teams, sits on a hill just north of the center of town. The wide expanse of grass serves well as the city's traditional spot for the annual burning.

After learning about this decidedly different ritual, born in the City Different no less, I gave some serious thought to the gloom I wanted to dispel. I came to the conclusion that I was ready to let go of a heaviness I felt in my heart. From as long as I could remember the emotional pain had been with me to a greater or lesser degree. It was something I had carried with me my whole life that manifested as a dull ache in my chest or a lump in my throat.

While I wasn't always aware of it, I remembered feeling it even as a child as young as ten. It caused me to hold myself back, observe, but not quite throw myself in the middle of the action at full tilt. I was not athletic, so I was always the last to be picked for any team sports; I was shy, so I usually didn't get asked to dance at school dances; I got good grades so didn't get into trouble; but I wasn't gregarious to stand out in any way, so I often went unnoticed by my peers as well as the adults in my world.

This invisibility led to the pain in the center of my chest. I wanted to shout to the world, "I exist. See me." But, day after day, year after year, until I left college for Colorado at age eighteen, I quietly followed the rules even though there was little joy in doing so.

There was a still small voice deep inside of me, as I

contemplated being free of this lifelong ache, which whispered to me of completing some sort of a cycle in Santa Fe and eventually moving on. Could there be some sort of force at play whereby I could let go of the depth of my pain and be able to leave it all behind me, both emotionally and also physically, by choosing to live somewhere else?

I knew I would be seeing Nellie at the Zozobra celebration and was determined to talk to her about it. Needless to say, as the day of the celebration arrived, I was filled with anticipation, both excited to see the marionette burn and also, on a more personal level, to use the event to move forward in my life.

I met up with Nellie and crew at 4 p.m. in a parking lot a mile or so from the park. The celebration would start in just a few hours, as soon as it got dark. The energy of the crowd was palpable as we joined a small group walking uphill toward the park. As we walked, the crowd began to swell.

Based on the sheer size and volume of the surging crowd that kept expanding around, I easily believe that the full 30,000 attendees predicted were turning out for the event. I felt like I was at a sporting event, a football game between rival teams that brought out the rowdiness in its spectators. We were joined by more and more people spilling over the sidewalk and into the street, which had been blocked off to traffic.

The park was uphill all the way. I panted as we strode briskly, keeping up with Nellie's kids who were practically running. They had grown in the four years since I had moved to Santa Fe. Aaron was thirteen. Kate and Willow were six and nine. These kids were dear to my heart and I was happy to spend this special evening with them.

"Let's see how close we can get to the front," Aaron hollered. It was hard to hear over the boisterous crowd.

"Keep me in view at all times, young man," Nellie cautioned as Aaron seemed ready to leave us all in the dust.

"Yeah, I know."

"And wait up for your sisters," Nellie said.

The younger girls were each wearing little backpacks, carrying sweaters and water bottles, I imagined. The two staples of living at a high altitude: water, because one was constantly getting dehydrated, and another layer of clothing, because the temperature always dropped by at least ten degrees once the sun went down.

Nellie was carrying a lightweight picnic basket. I had a backpack with some food in it, as well as water and warm clothes. We planned to have a picnic dinner on our blankets while waiting for the festivities to start.

Once we reached Fort Marcy Park at the top of the hill, there were throngs of people milling around, searching for the best place to lay down blankets and, yes, watch a huge puppet burn. Okay, I said to myself, why not?

It was then that I first glimpsed Zozobra from a distance way in front me at the far end of the park. Monstrous and dressed in white, with enormous arms flailing, he looked like a ghost with grotesque giant red sneering lips, big green eyes, and an ugly, pointy, beak-like nose. He seemed a fitting embodiment of doom and gloom.

After we got settled in on Nellie's Mexican blanket, I took the chance to catch up with Nellie while her kids horsed around and ate their picnic dinner.

"Okay, I'll get right to the point," I said. "I'm just not

sure how long I should stay in Santa Fe."

Nellie turned to look me straight in the eyes. I felt her presence bore into me like a laser beam. It was both disconcerting and reassuring at the same time. Disconcerting because she really knew me. Reassuring because she really cared about me.

"Don't *should* all over yourself, Sara," she said.

I laughed self-consciously. Yup, Nellie sure had my number all right. I was still the proper New England-raised, wanting to do what was right, kinda gal, through and through. And Nellie, in her abrupt one-liner had cut right through my blunt question as though she had seen it coming a long time ago. She probably knew, from the moment she took me out in the wilderness alone some five and a half years ago that at some point my time in Santa Fe would be up.

"Trust in the divine timing of everything. Know that when the time is right for you to move on from here to your next adventure, you will be sure."

Just then, her kids came racing up, shouting, laughing, and energized by the crowd. And that was that: beginning, middle, and end of my conversation with Nellie on the subject as she turned to give them her attention.

"Mom, can I have some money for a hat?" Aaron asked.

"I want one too," said Kate, the youngest.

"Mom, can I have a necklace?" asked Willow. There were vendors all over the place selling Zozobra paraphernalia, of all things. In addition to baseball caps and necklaces, I saw vendors walking around selling all sorts of trinkets that actually had nothing to do with the occasion but were simply Santa Fe mementos.

"You know I don't have the money for that stuff," Nellie said with resignation. "Sit down and finish your dinner."

Nellie glanced over at me and rolled her eyes just barely, as if to say she would love to keep chatting with me but was just unable to at that moment.

I nodded to signal I understood even though I was disappointed. I really wanted the chance to talk further to Nellie about this topic that was weighing heavily on me. Ultimately, though, it was completely up to me how long I stayed in Santa Fe. I knew it and Nellie did too. She and I were friends but were obviously on very different paths. I had the luxury and freedom to pack up and go as I saw fit, whenever and wherever I chose. She did not.

The kids sat down as they were told. I figured the walk had made them hungry.

We munched on cold chicken, carrot sticks, potato salad, and chips with salsa. We drank cold water from our water bottles and had some dark chocolate for dessert.

As dusk came over the grassy enclave, the crowd seemed to settle down. Far ahead of us, because we were in the middle of the park and not in the front after all, activity began to take place around the huge puppet, the height of a ten-story building.

After I finished eating, I wanted to take a walk down to the far end of the field to see what Zozobra looked like close up. Since Nellie had released me to come to my own conclusion about how long I should stay in Santa Fe, I knew I had to get serious about dropping my baggage This burning had a deeper meaning for me than simply a night out with friends.

"Who wants to come with me to check out Zozobra?"

I asked the kids. It turned out the older two did.

"Kate and I'll stay here and watch our stuff," Nellie said.

So, off the three of us went to view the effigy of doom and gloom that was to be burned that night.

The paper mâché puppet was even more intimidating from close up. We had to battle a lot of other picture takers and curiosity seekers to get a decent view. But he was about fifty feet tall and ugly. More like a caricature of the pictures I had seen in magazines. His eyes bulged out and his mouth was grotesque.

"Okay doom and gloom," I said silently to the statue. "I am more than ready to see you die for good."

Even if this was simply a silly Santa Fe–style carnival for tourists and locals, I was willing to suspend judgment and take this burning up of doom and gloom seriously.

Fire is universally regarded as a great purifier, I thought, as the phrase, "Phoenix rising from the ashes," went through my mind... to be followed by another well-known expression, "Trial by fire."

While I was not sure about the deep meanings behind these axioms, they reinforced the power inherent in the ritual of burning something up and, in the process, rendering it completely transformed.

"Let's head back to our spot," I said to the kids. It was beginning to get dark. They ran circles around me but followed my lead.

We walked briskly back to the blanket where Nellie and her youngest were putting away the picnic and getting bundled up against the inevitable coolness.

There was some live brass music playing by this time and city officials were making a few short speeches. It was muffled and I could barely hear them, but I understood that it was almost time to light the puppet on fire.

I could see on the stage a giant torch being raised into the air, which apparently was the signal to the crowd for silence. A hush filled the park that was now so packed with people that there was no more visible grass. The kids were sitting down and nestled together on the blanket. The girls' small warm bodies were comforting to me as I watched the puppet in awe.

All eyes were on the man with the torch. The feeling of anticipation reminded me of a Fourth of July fireworks display, just as the first fireworks were shot up into the air and right before they exploded into the sky.

The crowd then began chanting: "Burn him, Burn him." I joined in, jumping to my feet. "Burn him, burn him." I laughed and screamed with everyone else.

It was turning into a frenzied free-for-all when finally, the man touched the torch to Zozobra several times in several different places. When the effigy burst into flames, the area visibly brightened.

The flames grew larger and brighter. The crowd continued to roar with excitement, erupting into spontaneous clapping and revelry as though the home team had just scored a touchdown.

The kids were whooping and hollering. Caught up in the moment, I found myself cheering and clapping, my hands over my head, as I imagined the flames consuming my gloom.

I felt ready to let go of my woundedness that night at Zozobra. Let me claim an authentic life for myself full of passion, instead of merely a white bread existence.

As I lost myself in the energy of the night, I thought

back to other such occasions where I had truly let go. To my surprise, the night I met Michael was on top of the list. I remembered the energy I had felt dancing across from him and what a fantastic dancer he had been.

I had felt so alive those early months with Michael, full of the optimism of youth and new love. Those feelings came back to me the night of Zozobra. I was giddy, caught up in the frenzied revelry. Even if the occasion was somewhat manufactured and even silly, the affiliation with the other celebrants was intoxicating.

Weirdly, as Zozobra burned, he let out an eerie moaning sound.

"What the heck is that noise?" I asked Nellie.

"I don't know how they make him do that," she said. "But every year, he makes that God-awful groaning sound like he's really dying."

Maybe it was the type of wood, I thought, or wood that was slightly damp would make that creaking sound too as it was burning.

Regardless, I felt a palpable relief from my gloom. As I watched the burning, feeling myself to be part of a sea of vibrating onlookers, I felt really good. I could breathe freely and my heart felt open. I relaxed into the openness and smiled, feeling true happiness.

But, like all change, this shedding of gloom seemed to be incremental. And, as cathartic as it was to be there and witness the burning of Old Man Gloom, my ambivalence about remaining in Santa Fe had not been abated.

The marionette burned quickly. Made of dry timber and paper mâché, the spectacle seemed to lose its luster once the flames engulfed him. People began leaving before Zozobra was completely reduced to ashes. It had been a very high-energy event and I felt spent as we packed up our blanket and followed the crowd back down the way we had come.

I carried the picnic basket as Nellie carried her youngest on her back.

I had planned to try again to talk to Nellie on the walk back. But, with three exhausted and whiney kids to contend with, I just didn't have the heart to bring it up with her on the way back to our cars.

It was late and we were all spent. Ultimately, whether or not to move was my decision. Nellie's reluctance to discuss it made the fact I had to make this decision myself all the clearer to me that night.

I thought about the fact that she was unable to guide me, as I trudged down the hill, feeling detached suddenly from Nellie and her kids. I'd been lucky to have guides all along in Santa Fe—she'd been my first—and I was reluctant to make a move without a sounding board.

Nellie did say one more thing on the walk back that stayed with me. Coming up from behind and putting Kate down to walk a bit on her own, she took my arm and whispered, "Before you leave Santa Fe, you should consider spending some time with my friend Suzanne out on the Mesa."

Startled, I looked at her with a quizzical expression, but the moment had passed. I wondered if she had somehow read my mind but didn't want to spoil the moment by asking. We continued walking silently in the enveloping darkness.

Nellie's car was parked not too far from mine. I loaded her kids into their seats and hugged Nellie lightly. We said our tired goodbyes quickly.

As I was leaving, Nellie fixed me with her trademark soul-searching stare. "Trust in what you know, Sara."

And then she got into her car and started it.

I walked slowly toward my car. This night had ended the way many of my other out-of-the-ordinary experiences had ended in Santa Fe: with a high that seemed to reach the stars, only to have my mood crash dramatically shortly thereafter.

While I wasn't able to chat with Nellie about it further that night, the fact that a decision was looming ever closer, remained in my awareness in the weeks and months that immediately followed the festival of Zozobra.

Yes, life was hard in Santa Fe. But, like a cactus flower that blooms in the desert, one could come alive here in beautiful and mysterious ways. Born out of the hardship I had experienced, I was beginning to bloom from the inside out. A delicate, but very perceptible shift toward the light was taking place within me.

This made me wonder then, if I had come to Santa Fe for a reason, had I found what I was looking for? And, when would I know for sure? Did I "get" all the spirituality I needed from Santa Fe and could I take it out into the world with me?

Certainly, the heaviness in my heart felt significantly dissipated since I had identified the feeling earlier in the day and had symbolically given it up in the ceremonial burning of Zozobra. And, if my heart actually was lighter, perhaps I would be freed up to leave Santa Fe when the time came.

I balked at the thought, however, as I could not contemplate what lay beyond my current reality.

I imagined I was feeding on spiritual food that

sustained me for only a short period of time before I needed to ingest some more. Santa Fe was nourishing me in that unique way. People and experiences seemed to come to me out of nowhere that healed me and guided my inner journey. I didn't think I would be able to duplicate the connectedness I felt in Santa Fe anywhere else.

I wondered if I could find a way to sustain myself spiritually if I should leave.

A LESSON FROM THE GRANDMOTHERS

All honest work is good work; it is capable of leading to self-development, provided the doer seeks to discover the inherent lessons and makes the most of the potentialities for such growth.
~ Paramahansa Yogananda

During the weeks between Zozobra and calling Suzanne, I tried not to think too far ahead. While there were interesting aspects to my day-to-day existence, the adventures of a non-traditional nature, which were part of a larger spiritual quest, were more noteworthy.

Living in Santa Fe had connected me to other seekers, such as Mo and Emmy. I was exposed to books by seekers including, *The Road Less Traveled* by M. Scott Peck, M.D., and the *Seth Speaks* books by Jane Roberts, which I devoured.

In *The Road Less Traveled*, Scott Peck begins by saying, "Life is difficult. This is a Great Truth, one of the Greatest Truths." Upon reading those words of wisdom, I felt less alone.

I had grown up believing that life should be easy for someone like me: smart, pretty, middle class, with a good education and "a good head on your shoulders," as my mother always said. So, what went wrong? Why was I living a hand-to-mouth existence in a faraway city, divorced and directionless?

The answer that came to me after a while was that nothing was wrong. Yes, I was going through a difficult phase of my life, but others too had questioned, sought, and, as a result, embraced new inner and outer freedoms.

No, I was not alone in my isolation. Popular culture, it seemed, was filled with those whose alienation had propelled them into nontraditional lifestyles and, as a result, new awareness. In other words, "I was exactly where I was supposed to be," a phrase that was popular in Santa Fe.

In *Seth Speaks*, author Jane Roberts finds herself channeling information from Seth, an advanced entity with clear and insightful advice for us humans, calling him, "an energy personality essence no longer focused in the physical form." While I was skeptical at first about this concept, the open-mindedness I was getting in the habit of allowing since I had come to Santa Fe seemed to work for me in this case.

This entity had a consciousness that was not confined to a body. Okay, I thought, it's possible.

The theme running through my own life as well as through the books I was reading was that humans were emerging from our materialistic mindset into a more holistic sense of connectedness.

Whether through pop psychology, Eastern mysticism, or New Age channeling, the message was the same: life is not black and white. It is filled with gray areas, inconsistencies, mysteries. What we see in the physical world is not all there is. For centuries, people had believed in angels, Great Spirits, animal guides, energy. A resurgence was occurring in which personal experiences of spirituality were again being discussed and written about. And, this mirrored my personal experience.

Judaism and Christianity stressed reliance on rabbis, priests, or ministers to interpret God's will. In contrast, the older forms of spirituality that were becoming prevalent again, at least in some circles deemed New Age, stressed a personal experience of spirit that was tangible and available to all, regardless of church or dogma.

This appealed to me since I was beginning to have some deep feelings of connectedness with someone or something that felt very comforting to me. I realized that this feeling was what I had been seeking all my life... in my relationship with Michael, my pursuit of adventure and career, and my forays as a teenager into pot and drinking.

I had not been raised in any particular religion and had been taught from a very young age that physical reality was all that existed. I was both relieved and intrigued to learn firsthand that this was not necessarily true. The realization that I could actually have my own personal spiritual connection that I could tap into for strength and guidance took shape in my life.

This notion began to have greater significance and bear more weight for me as my time in Santa Fe lengthened. I noticed that when I got quiet inside, I could sometimes hear the whisper of a small voice that was my inner knowing making itself heard.

As things looked, I would go on about my days with little or no thought about life's bigger questions until I would get an inner nudge of some sort from my spiritual self that would signal it was time to take the next step. In this case, that meant calling Suzanne and setting up a time to visit her land.

It was early November. Fall and winter were generally

pretty mild in Santa Fe so walking outside was still feasible. After a few rings, a woman's voice answered. "Hello."

"Hi," I stammered. "You don't know me, but Nellie had suggested I give you a call... I'm a friend of Nellie's. Um, my name is Sara."

"Hi, Sara, I've been expecting your call," Suzanne said warmly. "Would you like to come by and visit my land?"

"Well, I am free this coming Sunday," I said tentatively.

"Great," Suzanne replied.

As we were talking, I thought to myself that I really had no clue why Nellie was pairing me up with this woman, though it was probably something to do with spirituality. I was wondering, while I had her on the line, if I should ask her what her spiritual "thing" was. But I dismissed that thought, because how do you ask someone such a question?

I didn't ask, but I thought that her spiritual leanings probably couldn't phase me at this point. After all, in Santa Fe I'd already been to see a shaman and an acupuncturist, as well as attended a Native American sweat lodge for women only. In addition, I'd experienced some more intangible forms of spirituality; animals as spirit guides, and people who may or may not have been supernatural in origin. Actually, what got me to move to Santa Fe in the first place was the one-night solo camp out and mini vision quest where I had fasted and, as a result, had a strong sense that I needed to be here, at least for a while.

So, six years later, out of a marriage and off any kind of traditional career path, here I was, again meeting someone new and venturing out onto the land for another "spiritual" adventure.

Suzanne proceeded to give me directions. It sounded something like this: "When you get to the Las Vegas exit, take it, and proceed about ten miles. Then you'll see a convenience store on your left and a dirt road on your right. Turn right onto the dirt road and proceed about half a mile until you come to a rundown shed on the righthand side of the road."

She told me that the road would fork to right after that. Then I would need to turn left at a row of mailboxes and proceed down the dirt road to the house.

"You will see it as soon as you turn at the mailboxes. It is a large white ranch-style home. Turn into the driveway and park. You'll likely notice several horses grazing outside in the adjacent fields."

Whew, I thought. This sounds iffy at best. Yet, I marveled at how accustomed I had become to tooling around the back roads of New Mexico in my little red Toyota Tercel hatchback.

This life was nothing I had foreseen in my wildest dreams. Once the fear of being in Santa Fe had receded a bit after my first couple of years, I had begun to love the freedom of the wide-open spaces and to draw inspiration from the unspoiled beauty that was all around me every day.

"I'll do my best to be there by noon on Sunday," I said to Suzanne from my end of the phone.

"I'll be on the lookout for you around then," she said. "My dogs will likely come out to greet you when they see you drive up. But, don't worry, they are very friendly."

I thanked her and upon hanging up, looked over my cryptic notes on which I had scribbled directions to Suzanne's place. I figured I could find it all right if I paid close enough attention to the landmarks she had pointed out.

The morning of my visit to Suzanne's, I packed my backpack with what I had begun to think of as *Santa Fe Essentials*: water bottle, hat, sunblock, and fleece jacket. I usually threw a pair of jeans in the back seat along with a down vest, just in case. I put on shorts, a tee-shirt, and my Tevas, good walking sandals. I was all set.

As I drove out of town, once again I let my mind unwind into the vastness of the landscape. I would sure miss this place if I were to leave, I thought. And then I remembered the conversation that had taken place between Nellie and myself a couple weekends ago at Zozobra. Or, more realistically, the lack of conversation.

The only thing Nellie had mentioned was to go visit Suzanne. Nellie always talked to me about gaining a connection to spirit through the land, which I assumed was why she had directed me toward Suzanne.

I surmised that I needed to connect more fully with the land here in this part of the world, absorb whatever energy was there for me to absorb, and then move on elsewhere, renewed.

No, more than renewed, I thought—totally transformed.

However, I wanted to know for sure that the time was right to go. I wanted to be certain that I was complete with being in Santa Fe before I left. Yet, how would I know these things?

I decided on that drive that I was ready to meet my destiny: moving into the world at large as a spiritual being. I was ready to be someone who was attuned to the subtler aspects of energy.

I had become a woman who could draw sustenance from nature, trust others who were very different from myself, and keep an open mind about customs and beliefs that were completely foreign to those I had been raised with.

Living in Santa Fe had taught me all that, and as I drove an hour or so out to Suzanne's land that late November, it felt right and good.

I careened down the smooth highway, looking out over a barren landscape of dry sagebrush, doing my best to follow Suzanne's directions. I had them written in cryptic shorthand on a sticky note that lay beside me on the passenger seat. When I had first arrived in Santa Fe, I would have been mortified at trying to find a ranch out in the middle of nowhere with weird directions citing natural landmarks instead of street signs as markers. Initially, I got lost a lot.

That was another thing about living in Santa Fe that had changed me. I had gotten used to paying more attention to what was around me: trees, rocky outcroppings, dilapidated buildings, and mile markers between two otherwise nondescript points on a map.

I had grown up with street signs, well-marked highways, and well-lit exits. Everything had been very civilized in New England. Property that was on the verge of collapse would be condemned and then torn down. Nothing was left to decay and weather like you'd find on the back roads outside Santa Fe where abandoned 100-year-old structures were often found in various stages of collapse, left entirely to the elements.

Now, I was used to this way of life. Just at the point at which I was thinking of leaving, I realized that this life had started to suit me just fine. I had become more confident in not having all the answers. In fact, not only was I in limbo in terms of not knowing exactly where I was going, as I hit the road to Suzanne's place, but, in general I was in limbo at this point in time. I didn't know how long I would stay in Santa Fe and where I would go if and when I left. But it was okay.

In the past I would have been a nervous wreck trying to force a solution. Now, I was content to let things unfold organically. I figured I would know when I knew. In the meantime, I was driving down a beautiful road on a gorgeous day, going on another adventure. What a joy.

After about forty-five minutes, I realized I had reached the Las Vegas, New Mexico, exit. Game on, I thought. Time to pay attention. I tracked the ten miles from the exit and kept my eyes peeled for the fork in the road, check; the row of mailboxes, check; the farmhouse visible from the turnoff, check. And sure enough, there were three huge dogs running out to greet my car.

As I pulled up, I suddenly felt keyed up and nervous. I had never met Suzanne, after all, and really had no idea what to expect.

A woman came out of the house and called to the dogs. Dressed in jeans and work boots, Suzanne smiled at me and offering me her hand. She was big; a large, loud, no-nonsense kind of woman with a firm handshake that felt like a man's.

"So nice to meet you, Sara," she said at once. Suzanne was in her early sixties. I knew from Nellie that she had raised three boys in Southern California and was widowed. She had been living out on this barren patch of arid desert all alone for several years.

"You too," I said. Feeling a bit unsure about what to talk about, I had the good sense to keep my mouth shut and agree to let Suzanne show me around her ranch.

We stopped briefly in the kitchen to get some doggie treats for the dogs and water and sunblock for us humans. Then we gathered her dogs together and set out for a walk around her land.

We walked the length of her property and Suzanne pointed out certain landmarks. She spent her time mending fences and potholes, caring for her animals and occasionally seeing clients at a battered women's shelter in Las Vegas. Suzanne was trained as a therapist and had gravitated to more alternative forms of work, including rebirthing.

As we walked, I was enjoying the early winter sunshine and marveling at the endless miles of open space all around me.

I began to think about my childhood again and how different it had been in every way from what I was experiencing now. Life then was ordered, rigid, and hard. That was it. Period.

Today, life was unpredictable, wild, and wonderful, filled with emotion, both high and low, and filled with promise. How had this transformation taken place and when?

I laughed to myself.

The dogs were veering off the dirt road and Suzanne followed, motioning me to join her. Very shortly we climbed a small hill and sat down on some rocks. We were surrounded by three pine trees, which formed a perfect circle around the spherical flat rock where we sat. I felt like I had entered a small green room that had appeared almost magically out of nowhere, sheltered from the wind.

I marveled at the evenness of the spacing of the trees that had grown there naturally, surrounding the rock. A sense of peacefulness overtook me.

"I call this place Three Pine Hill," Suzanne said. "I just love the energy here."

I felt a jolt of recognition. Nellie had wanted me to experience the land. Maybe it was a piece of the puzzle I needed to complete my Santa Fe journey.

My mind began to move very fast; thoughts raced through my head about the spiritual geography of the land in northern New Mexico and the possibility that there really was a sort of "energy vortex" there, as Mo had been explaining to me just recently. She had said that certain people were drawn to the land for healing.

"You can't feel the energy if you're too busy thinking," Suzanne said then, seeming to read my mind. "Just sense it."

I tried to engage her in conversation, feeling panic for no reason.

There was nothing to focus my attention on. No sounds: radio, TV, people talking; No shapes or colors, only the greenish-gray of the flat landscape, melting into a green-blue sky that went on forever. What a distance one needed to go in this day and age to get away from the pervasive sights and sounds of modern life.

The stillness and space threatened to engulf me. I feared for my life. I feared for my sanity. I wanted to talk— just about anything or nothing, simply to break the silence that seemed ominous and all-pervasive.

I took a couple of deep breaths in an attempt to ground myself. I looked down at my feet, noticing dusty socks sticking out of mud-caked walking sandals. I wanted to avoid the somewhat creepy sensation that was sweeping over me.

But Suzanne was ruthless. She didn't want to make small talk about her grandchildren or my job. "Listen" was all she said and wandered off a bit, leaving me momentarily alone on Three Pine Hill.

I dared to breathe. All was still and quiet. All was vast and open. All was peaceful and, yes, perfect. Perfect in its mystery and perfect in its beauty.

Then I heard voices in the wind. Female voices laughing and talking wildly. Ancient voices speaking Spanish and English. Or was it the wind whipping through the pine trees, or squirrels scampering, or Suzanne calling to the dogs and beckoning me onward, saying it was time to return to her cabin. Or maybe it was my imagination.

We resumed our walk and didn't speak for a while. Suzanne seemed not to notice as I wiped tears from my cheeks. Then we did make small talk that wasn't small. Suzanne told me about the Grandmothers whose spirits were the caretakers of the land.

"The Grandmothers lived and died on this plateau, more than a hundred years ago," Suzanne said as we walked. "They've witnessed bloodshed and destruction, domination and forced submission, the births of their children, the deaths of their husbands, and yet they prevail to watch over their domain for generations to come."

Okay, I thought. I had been reading the Seth material and thinking about non-physical entities. I had also been wondering if the soul really was separate from the body and, if so, did consciousness exist before and after death.

There I was, getting my own experience of just this

very thing. I thought about the possibility of spirits of those who had lived and died on this land remaining close by. Chills ran up and down my spine.

"What will happen if the land is purchased and developed by out-of-state moguls from the East or West coasts?" I asked.

"I shudder to think," Suzanne said.

We continued the walk back to her home in silence. This time the quiet was comforting and serene. The spirits of the Grandmothers seemed to envelop me in their loving presence. As we got further and further away from Three Pine Hill, their presence seemed to dissipate until it was completely gone.

When we arrived back at the house, Suzanne asked me if I wanted to try rebirthing before going into Las Vegas for lunch.

I thought about it. I had been hearing of friends in Santa Fe experiencing rebirthing sessions. Supposedly, one could actually go back to one's birth memories, to release what Rebirthers referred to as birth trauma, early impressions upon the brain and nervous system that could influence one's worldview into adulthood. For example, one could feel like the world is a scary place at birth and that feeling could influence one's life in subtle and not-so-subtle ways for decades, according to Rebirthing philosophy.

"I'm not sure," I said. I felt like I had gone through enough for one day with the encounter with the spirits of the Grandmothers on Three Pine Hill.

"I know it seems a bit much after our... um... walk," Suzanne said. "But the rebirthing experience can help to smooth things out."

Suzanne then told me a little about her social work practice in Southern California and how she had morphed into doing rebirthing in New Mexico.

"I realized the mind can only take one so far in terms of their own healing," she said. "The body itself contains a cellular memory that is accessed through the Rebirthing process. The deep emotional imprints can then be released."

"I guess so," I said. While I had been reading the Seth books and contemplating the reality of the Spirit world, the brief encounter with the Grandmothers had unnerved me. It had come so quickly and gently that I hadn't reacted at all outwardly. But, safely back in Suzanne's house, I had begun to feel a bit woozy.

"It's actually pretty relaxing," Suzanne reassured me.

That sounded good to me. "Okay," I said. "I actually do need to relax a bit right now."

"That's completely understandable," Suzanne said with a sympathetic smile. "Let's get started."

She led me into a small room off her living room and closed the door behind us. She instructed me to lie down on a single-size futon on the floor and, after lighting candles and incense, and putting on some soothing New Age music, sat down on a pillow beside me. Suzanne then instructed me in circular breathing, the trademark of Rebirthers.

"Let the breath flow in naturally on its own without forcing it," she said. "And on the exhale, let go all the way."

As I lay on the futon, covered up with blankets and quilts, listening to even tones coming from Suzanne's cassette player, I felt tears well up inside me.

"Don't resist the emotions," Suzanne instructed. "Just

let them come."

I had a memory of being in ballet class when I was about eight years old. I wore a pale pink tutu, tights, and ballet shoes, also pale pink. The studio was large and empty except for a barre that ran along the back wall. The front wall was covered with a floor-to-ceiling mirror. The room was brightly lit with a wooden floor.

About a dozen girls lined up, with our right hands holding onto the barre and watched ourselves practice in the mirror. I felt clumsy and fat although I am quite certain I was neither one. I kept hearing my ballet teacher telling me to hold my stomach in; not to let my stomach stick out.

And I watched myself shutting down my joy. Hearing again the adults around me saying she's too serious... such a reserved child... Maybe I just wanted to dance freely without thinking about my stomach. Maybe I just wanted to laugh loudly and twirl around the room making up my own dance steps.

Instead, I heard: "*Relevé, plié,*" over and over as I did first position, second position, third position, fourth position, and fifth position, straining to get it right. But always not quite hitting the mark.

After I sobbed for a little while, Suzanne asked me to tell her what I was experiencing.

"I could never really be myself as a child," I said finally, my head feeling dizzy and my body tingling then numb.

"Keep breathing," Suzanne said.

Soon I began to sense a gentle presence all around me. It was the same fluttering and light breeze that I had felt at Three Pine Hill. This time I recognized them. The Grandmothers, it seemed, had returned. And, lying close to the earth in Suzanne's sunroom on the land, I heard the

Grandmothers' message:

"For far too long, humankind has been trying to force its will upon the planet. We are advocates of this small corner of the earth and we are here to impress upon all who find themselves here that this land is not to be destroyed. It is sacred and it is powerful and to develop it would cause great harm to the animals and spirit beings who call it their home."

I saw a vision of a long, winding river and, within it, many faces of women, young and old, all with long wispy hair. The Grandmothers: the Custodians of the Land.

As I kept breathing and reporting to Suzanne what I was seeing and hearing she nodded in approval.

"They're really dear, aren't they?" she asked.

I was startled. But Suzanne said the Grandmothers came often to talk to her clients.

She asked them then if they had a message for me before they departed, these sweet, gentle old spirits who had sacrificed so much, and they said to me: "Your path will take you far away from New Mexico, but you will carry your experiences here with you forever in your heart."

And they were gone.

Suzanne instructed me to begin to breathe normally and to stretch my arms and legs to increase the circulation. I felt like I was being roused a deep sleep in which I had been dreaming intensely but, upon awakening, couldn't clearly remember the details of the dream.

I came out of the session and rose, feeling calm. I also realized I was suddenly ravenous.

Suzanne and I drove into Las Vegas for lunch. I rode shotgun in her beat up old pick up and a couple of her dogs came along, bobbing up and down in the back, their ears pinned back by the wind, their noses alert to the scents of the dust and the highway. When we got to town, Suzanne didn't bother to lock the truck doors.

"There's nothing in here anybody could possibly want," she said with a wink. "Besides if somebody wants to steal this piece of junk, they can have it. They'd be doing me a favor. The insurance on this thing is worth more than the truck itself."

Somehow, I sensed no self-respecting stranger would venture within arm's distance of the truck with the dogs lazily sprawled out in back. Although they were sweet, Lucy was half wolf and Kiowa was a husky. Both were large-statured and could fool anybody into thinking they were ferocious watchdogs.

We entered a diner just off Main Street that looked like it came straight off the set of a John Wayne Western. Little cactuses in mauve clay pots lined the windowsills, otherwise caked with a layer of dust. Plastic window shades hung down over the spotted panes, blocking out the ever-pervasive New Mexico sunlight. Inside the diner, all was dark and cool and quiet. Waitresses didn't move too fast. They didn't have to. Their customers weren't in a hurry to go anywhere. There was nowhere to go for miles.

We slid into a booth and Suzanne ordered for both of us. "You've got to try the house specialty," she said. "Sour cream enchiladas."

Although I was somewhat concerned about the over-abundance of calories, coupled with a lack of vegetables and roughage, I kept my mouth shut and let it go. My openness to new ideas, concepts, not to mention foods and people, was expanding.

A couple of guys in cowboy hats and jeans, who had

just finished eating, got up and sauntered over to the counter to pay their bill. Real life Marlboro men, I thought; ranchers trying to eke out a meager living off the parched desert land. Or maybe they were wealthy movie stars who had bought ranches out here to get away from the Hollywood lifestyle.

What did it matter? New Mexico was the grand equalizer. To survive here was no easy feat. Living here had provided us all with a common denominator, a shared thread, weaving us all together like a Navajo rug.

With that my enchiladas arrived. And wow were they fabulous. As I ate the warm, blue corn tortillas stuffed with soft melted cheese and sour cream, smothered with homemade green chile, I couldn't help but think about the Grandmothers' message.

I had just gotten a definitive answer to the question that I was pondering. It had become clear that the Grandmothers thought I would be leaving Santa Fe. Now what, I wondered. Would I be able to make a spiritual life elsewhere?

The spirituality of the land, people, and unique history of this part of the world had made a deep and lasting impression upon me, that much was clear. What I had yet to determine was whether or not other places could also nurture me in a similar way. And how was I going to take what I had absorbed here with me.

I didn't take off for home until sunset. I had to go to work at the publishing company the next morning and it seemed like I had a long week ahead of me with a lot to think about. As I eased my car onto the highway and watched the big sky slowly darken, I knew in my heart that my time to depart Santa Fe was growing ever closer.

This thought was both reassuring and terrifying.

LETTING IN A LITTLE MORE LIGHT

As far as we can discern, the sole purpose of human existence is to kindle a light in the darkness of mere being.
~ Carl Jung

After my trip to Suzanne's land, I began to think seriously about what was to come next for me. I had moved to Santa Fe when I was twenty-seven years old hoping to jumpstart my life with my new husband Michael. But things hadn't gone as planned.

At this point, I was thirty-three and had been divorced for five years. I had given up doing massage therapy and pursued my dream career: writing. This was made manifest through a gradual progression of several jobs. I was an administrative assistant and calendar editor for the *Santa Fe Magazine*, a trendy arts and entertainment publication.

At some point, I transitioned from there to becoming employed as the desktop publisher for a small local book publishing company. I had also begun to interview visual and healing artists for local publications on the side.

Internally, I had adjusted to single life. My self-esteem had improved, as life had brought me deep friendships and meaningful experiences.

After listening to the Grandmothers' message, my

focus had ever so slightly leaned toward moving away from Santa Fe. I was open, for the first time since I had arrived, to taking the next step in my journey.

Rather than trying to force an outcome, i.e. where to go and when, I decided to let the answer come to me of its own accord. I refused to get overly anxious by trying to figure out where to go and what to do by analyzing things to death. Throughout my whole life, I had the habit of overthinking problems. This time, I was determined not to go there.

Okay. I had learned something over the past six years. Before Santa Fe, I would have struggled to get an answer. I would have demanded an answer from myself based on empirical reasoning. I would have thought myself into a quandary and, when thinking a thing to death wouldn't work, I would have spiraled into worry, anxiety, and even despair.

I no longer chose to live that way, thankfully. I was able to calmly ask the universe for guidance and, every day, believe wholeheartedly in the fact that the answer would appear when it was time.

One theme that kept emerging for me was the desire to go back to school to study writing or communication seriously and to make a career in that field. So, I started researching graduate schools simply out of curiosity. I figured I could go to grad school somewhere that I might actually like to live and stay there upon completion.

One thing I was sure of was, I didn't want to return to the Northeast. My home was not there anymore. Once I had left the rigid mindset of those I had grown up with and experienced the freedom of living out West, I was sold.

I started looking at Colorado, then, because I had gone

to massage school in Boulder more than ten years prior.

I had loved Colorado, so why not make it my home? I found a school in Denver, the University of Denver, that met my criteria: 1) It was in Colorado, and 2) It offered a master's degree in Communication.

Denver was a city, but it was located out West and at the foothills of the Rocky Mountains. This was a compromise between my childhood and my Santa Fe detour. I was hoping I'd have the opportunity to find meaningful work during the week and still be able to escape to the mountains during the weekends. The best of both worlds would allow me to actually have a career after all and hopefully, not have to live from hand-to-mouth into my thirties and beyond.

Most of my childhood friends had nest eggs already; not just savings accounts but retirement monies that were invested and poised to grow. I had neither. The whole time I lived in Santa Fe, I was unable to save any money; albeit not for lack of frugality. There just wasn't a whole lot of money to be earned and what living I did manage to eke out simple covered my basic living expenses and no more, period.

I was thirty-four.

It was time to make a change. I was not too old to go to graduate school or to make the move from New Mexico to Colorado.

I needed to call my parents and tell them about my plans, I thought. I was sitting in my ground-level apartment, looking out at my little patio. Everything had turned dry and brown. Winter was approaching.

I wondered what they would say about my decision to go to grad school and about my decision to stay out West.

Would they try to talk me into coming back East? I was firm in my feelings to not go back into what was familiar but unsatisfying but to move forward, somehow trusting in the unknown and in my desire for a deeply fulfilling life.

I wanted my parents to understand. Inside there was the little girl who was still seeking their approval. I dialed the phone and listened to it ring on the other end.

"Mom," I said after hearing her hello. "I'm thinking of going to graduate school this coming fall."

I took a deep breath after the words spilled out.

"What?" she asked, not sure she was hearing me correctly yet happily speechless for a moment.

"Yeah, I've been looking into UD in Denver, maybe getting my master's in Communication."

"Oh," she said as the news sunk in that I wouldn't be coming home to attend the University of Rhode Island.

"That's wonderful, Sara," she added, catching herself and wanting to be encouraging no matter what. After all, this was graduate school I was talking about here.

"Thanks. I'll let you know what I find out about the program and stuff," I said, throwing out a bone that I was at least including her somehow in my life's big decisions.

However, it was obvious to us both that my time in Santa Fe had all but severed that cord of emotional dependency between us.

"I'll put Dad on," she said.

"Hi, Dad," I said.

"Hello, great news I overheard about you applying to grad school," he said.

"Yeah, I thought I'd check out the University of Denver."

"Great, great," he said again. "Let us know how we can

help."

"I will," I said. And we said our goodbyes. But the interaction felt hollow, somehow.

There were words unsaid: I would not be moving back East; I would not be coming home; I was moving on, further from the place I had spent my childhood and further from my roots.

I looked around at my sparsely furnished apartment. Second-hand furniture filled the place: a wood-block coffee table from a yard sale, a couple of sand-colored couches donated by a friend who had gotten married and no longer needed them. Framed posters lined the walls— replicas of paintings done by local artists, some of whom I had even met.

Home Sweet Home, I thought. It was bittersweet. Bitter because of its simplicity and sweet for the same reason. Besides, home is where the heart is, right? I said to myself in defense of my humble abode.

I began the application process to the University of Denver's Master of Communication program. I took the Graduate Record Exam. I waited and, in that waiting thought a lot about my past.

Trips east had become increasingly stressful. I often ended up feeling like an oddity, someone who had taken a decidedly different turn in life than my contemporaries. And, different can sometimes trigger fear, confusion and distrust in others who cling to the familiar at all cost.

Case in point: one of the last times I had gone back home, I was hanging out with some friends I had grown up with who were talking about their entry-level salaries. My friends Gwen, Rich, and I were seated in a hazy bar that reeked of stale beer and greasy food.

Rich had majored in Zoology but had moved to New York to become a commodities trader on Wall Street. "Now that I'm a trader, we'll be able to send our kids to private schools," Rich bragged.

Apparently, he was making a ton of money on the stock exchange and was engaged to marry a woman from Long Island who had come from a wealthy family.

We were upper-middle-class kids whose parents were university professors, for the most part. But Rich had definitely moved up a notch or two on the socio-economic ladder and he wanted us to know all about it.

"I don't know why, but I let my parents talk me into going to med school," Gwen said. "Now I have three years of residency ahead of me before I can even earn enough to start paying off my student loans."

I felt small and insignificant, in spite of my time spent in Santa Fe. I had no large salary, nor lofty goals to share with my hometown friends over drinks.

"Well, I've been taking a bit of a detour," I said quietly.

Rich and Gwen looked up with confused expressions.

"I've been married and that wasn't all it was cut out to be. So, I'm just kind of hanging out in Santa Fe right now."

Rich and Gwen looked at me again; this time with utterly blank expressions. Gwen quickly changed the subject.

We said our goodbyes shortly thereafter. The light hugs and the shallow "see ya laters," didn't touch the sense of alienation that threatened to engulf me.

Our visit had ended on a superficial note; each of us wishing the other well. I had received no encouragement for my life's choice. Nor, had I experienced commonality of purpose among those I had grown up with. I was, it seemed, quite on my own.

I had begun to tell people I had grown up with—friends and extended family—that I had simply taken a "detour" through Santa Fe. This answer was usually in response to the questions I would get like, how long do you plan to stay there; what kind of career path does Santa Fe offer you; how's the dating scene there, etc. So, I came up with the detour explanation that seemed to cover all those bases and many others as well.

I wasn't really taking time out from anything. I was simply living my life in a nontraditional way. But, from the outside looking in, people could relate to the concept that sooner or later, I would "get back on track" and head into a more "mainstream" lifestyle.

Maybe yes, maybe no, I realized. But what did it matter as long as I was able to articulate my experiences in Santa Fe in a way that satisfied those who probably couldn't relate to what I was doing? According to many of my contemporaries, the traditional path of college, career, marriage, homeownership, and kids by the time one had reached their mid-thirties had obviously passed me by.

Or, maybe I was the one who had passed it all by on my detour through Santa Fe. I was headed somewhere else, it seemed, whether of my own choosing or simply happenstance, the luck of the draw, or fate.

As the year came to a close, I made the decision to stay in Santa Fe during Christmastime. I would not go "home" to Rhode Island for the holidays. The decision to stay in Santa Fe for the holidays represented closing the door metaphorically on my childhood and the lifestyle that was laid out before me by my parents, schools, upbringing and society.

When I called to tell them, I wouldn't be going home for the holidays, my parents had asked me if I would feel lonely staying in Santa Fe on my own. I realized I would probably feel lonelier when surrounded by family than I would be amongst my newfound tribe of misfits in the City Different.

I was reminded of a time long beforehand when a therapist had said to me, "There you were, surrounded by your parents and siblings, but just so alone."

This was my first Christmas away from my family. I had remained the dutiful daughter and had dedicatedly gone home for the holidays, even dragging Michael with me when had been together. This year was different.

There I was, feeling a little guilty for not going back to visit my parents, but determined to have a great Christmas in Santa Fe. In addition to the guilt, I felt scared. What if there was nothing outside the boundary of my childhood? What if I had been living an illusion for these past six years? What if I just curled up in a ball and cashed it all in for familiar and secure? No, I'd come too far, I thought.

Rather than wait until I had all the outside trappings of a home of my own, family and the Christmas tree, I felt complete enough within myself to just go for it and celebrate my own way, in my rental apartment, in my temporary city of residence with a likely short-term, though ever-so-dear friend Emmy. Short-term because I could never see myself living like Emmy—on the land—roughing it year after year and romancing an earlier, simpler time.

Emmy had decided to come to town for the big night, Christmas Eve. She had agreed to be around other people for a change instead of hibernating and isolating. So, it was to be a liberating time for both of us: Emmy because she realized she did, in fact, crave contact with other human beings, even if only occasionally. Me, because I wanted to see what celebrating my own brand of the holidays would feel like.

Emmy arrived at my apartment at 6 p.m. Bundled up against the dry chilly air, we decided we would drive as close to Canyon Road as we could get, park, and just start walking. Neither Emmy nor I had done the "*farolito* walk" before (small, sand-filled, paper bags illuminated with votive candles line the historic neighborhood streets and adobe walls), but it was a well-known local event, as much a Santa Fe tradition as Zozobra.

"Climb in," I said.

"Okay, I'm freezing," she said, getting into the front seat. "The heat's not working in my truck."

"Yikes."

"It's all right. I have a couple wool blankets and my parka."

While I admired her, I knew I was not like her in the fundamental sense that I was seeking some sort of balance between a spiritual and material existence. While I loved being close to the land and away from technology, a part of me wanted what the fast-paced, modern world had to offer: creativity, stimulation, excitement. The key for me was to find moderation and not get lost in the bells and whistles of a high-tech lifestyle. I also didn't want to become so immersed in a search for meaning that the spiritual trappings of Santa Fe became all-encompassing, obscuring reasonable material comforts.

"Let's do this," I said as I started the engine and

cranked up the heat.

"Yup," Emmy said.

We both laughed nervously. I wondered if she would be good company. She was a self-professed loner who didn't give a hoot about the holidays. And yet, I had chosen to spend my first Christmas away from home with her. What was I thinking? Mild panic was beginning to set in but I took a few deep breaths and drove stoically to the art district of Canyon Road.

The new moon was crescent-shaped in the clear dark sky.

I got as close to Canyon Road as I could, in spite of all the pedestrians and car traffic.

"Man, I feel claustrophobic already," Emmy said.

She was bundled up in a parka, hunched down in the passenger seat, a scarf wrapped around her neck and a round wool hat pulled down over her forehead, almost covering her eyebrows.

"Come on," I pleaded. "Let's just check it out since we're here already."

We parked, got out of the car and started walking. The shopkeepers, gallery owners, and residents of Canyon Road had placed candles inside paper bags and lit them. The *farolitos* lined the entire neighborhood for blocks and hoards of people had gathered to take in the scene. Once we arrived at the base of Canyon Road, throngs of others were already there and had formed small groups that were wandering through the winding neighborhood, singing Christmas carols.

"This looks a good place to start," I said.

"Yup," Emmy said again.

I couldn't get a read on her feelings. Was she okay,

ready to bolt, enjoying herself... but this wasn't the time to check in with her. It was dark, crowded, and cold.

As Emmy and I walked, we were joined by dozens of other walkers. Many carried lit candles to ward off the darkness. The shops and galleries were all holding open houses and most had placed complimentary paper cups of hot chocolate or sugar cookies out for the carolers. We joined in, stopped at the shops, sang carols, and moved on. The crowd was full of good cheer. We joined in a rendition of "Silent Night."

"I can't believe I'm doing this," Emmy said

"Singing Christmas carols, you mean?"

"Yeah, doing this whole holiday thing with all these people I don't even know."

"I know, me neither." Actually, I was beginning to enjoy myself. What was going on with Emmy became less of an issue, as I relaxed into the night and took in the lights and ambiance.

"My mom always bakes a ham on Christmas, and we have about fifty of my closest relatives for dinner every year," Emmy said.

I was relieved that Emmy was communicating finally.

"I've been going home for Christmas ever since I left home at eighteen," I said. "Even though we don't do the traditional holiday thing, the whole family is always together."

Emmy and I walked in silence for a few minutes, each of us lost in Christmases past.

I thought about my eclectic religious upbringing. We celebrated both the Christian and Jewish holidays since my parents were different religions. But they were also atheists and intellectuals. God did not exist for them in any context. The world was material only, not spiritual or mystical. This was my undoing as a kid.

I was naturally metaphysical and had no vocabulary or outlet for my core belief that everything was somehow connected and that there was a power greater than myself that was caring for me and guiding me if I tapped into it.

I was actually experiencing that inner connection as I wandered through the cold darkness with a crowd of happy carolers.

"Hey, you guys want candles?" said an anonymous voice ahead of us. I looked around. Just about everyone we were walking with had tiny white candles mounted on paper cups. The makeshift candle holders shielded the flames from any breeze.

"Sure," I said. There were a couple of people giving away the candles and cups. Emmy and I caught up to the voice and we each graciously took a white candle and a paper cup.

"Just peel down the sides until there is just a little circle around the candle," a woman instructed us. We did as we were told.

"Here, need a light?" she asked, holding her own candle out for us to light ours. We lit our candles and dripped a little wax on the bottom of the cup and then mounted the candle on it. Once the wax dried, it stuck and we could walk on, carrying lit candles. We were each holding little flames that illuminated a tiny space around each person.

I looked around me and saw a sea of tiny golden lights. I looked beyond to the street, the shops, the horizon, and the deep black sky with pinpricks of stars. I felt the light of the moment penetrate deep inside me. The kindness of strangers and the good in humanity warmed my heart.

We kept on going, following the crowd, stopping when they stopped, and singing when they sang, until we reached the end of the street. The *farolito* walk ended at the end of Canyon Road.

Emmy and I headed back to my apartment. About half a dozen duplexes surrounded the parking area. Not a soul was in sight. It was after 11 p.m., very dark and quiet.

Wherever I go, I thought, I'll miss the darkness and quietness of night. Most urban areas are noisier and more artificially lit these days. I just hoped I'd be able to adjust.

Emmy followed me to my front door, and, as I unlocked it, she fished out her car keys.

"Do you want to come in?" I asked.

Emmy shook her head. "That was really cool, though," she said, reaching out to give me a hug.

"Yeah. It was great," I said, patting her on the back. "Are you sure you don't want to stay over and drive back tomorrow?"

"No. I gotta feed my dogs, cats, and horses," she said. And we both laughed, knowing full well that Emmy could only stand to be in town for a couple of hours at any given time, max.

"You know, I'm thinking of leaving Santa Fe," I ventured.

Emmy looked at me quizzically for a second, then a wave of comprehension washed over her face.

"Better you than me, Sara," she said. "I just can't handle city life. All this technology hasn't made things any better, in my opinion."

I laughed but thought to myself that Emmy was too extreme in her rejection of all things modern.

Emmy went into a mini tirade then about how TV was a total waste of time and who needed news anyway when all of it was so negative. Our food supply was getting polluted with chemicals, which was why she was growing her own food for the most part. And the political system was such a bunch of bullshit that she never voted anyway.

Suddenly I was in a hurry for her to leave, even though I knew that her truck had no heat. Her negativity was draining me, and I wanted to hold onto the little bit of bliss I had experienced on the walk.

"Emmy," I said at length, "it's getting late."

"I know, Sara," she said. "Thanks for inviting me, and Merry Christmas."

"You too," I said. We hugged each other goodbye.

Emmy then climbed into her cold truck and pulled away.

I watched her go and waved.

I wasn't sure if Emmy had enjoyed the evening, but I definitely had. There had been something about the homegrown celebration that I found really satisfying; It was just good, honest fun with very little pretense. And it was available to all.

I went inside my apartment, feeling happily warmed and also, very tired. I settled in for the night.

I began to wonder if Emmy had succumbed to a conspiracy theory of some sort. If so, she and I were, in fact, quite different, as were our individual reasons for living in Santa Fe.

I had taken a detour but was coming around the bend to the other side. She had made a permanent lifestyle change and was completely locked into it. As, it seemed, were many others I had met here.

Emmy had not asked why I wanted to leave or where I wanted to go. Both she and Nellie had avoided talking about my choosing to move elsewhere. Or maybe they felt abandoned. Santa Fe was where those on the fringes of society felt at home. It united us oddballs and made us feel okay about being different.

If I returned to life outside, I could no longer claim that badge of honor. Would I be giving up everything I had gained over the past seven years?

I went inside my apartment and breathed a sigh of relief. I had done it; I had a Christmas Eve of my own. Celebrated my way and it felt just fine, thank you.

EAST MEETS WEST

In my own life I know that my state of cheerfulness is a reliable gauge of my level of spiritual enlightenment at that moment. The more cheerful, happy, contented, and satisfied I am feeling, the more aware I am of my deep connection to spirit.

~ Wayne Dyer

The winter passed. I began to think more seriously about attending the University of Denver the following fall. I would remain out West. That much was clear. There was no going back, only forward, taking my new self with me.

This slant toward Denver jibed with my new decision-making process. I simply let the idea hover around in my awareness without trying to push it one way or the other into being the "right" path. Day by day, an inner knowing got progressively stronger that this was meant to be.

One early spring day, my neighbor Mo and I were hanging out at the Lighthouse, catching up with each other and drinking our favorite lattes, when a flyer caught my eye.

Mo was about to sit down.

"Hey, check this out," I called.

She gingerly placed her steaming latte, along with what looked to be an almond croissant, on a nearby table. Then she came over to look at the bulletin board. We stood together and stared. Both of us were mesmerized by the countenance of a round woman with a moon-like face from the country of India.

The flyer said she was called Amachi, the Divine Mother. Ama, as she was known by her followers in India, was coming to Santa Fe to host meetings in a large enclosed tent on someone's land. The meetings, the flyer said, were called *Satsangs*, a Sanskrit word meaning "sacred gathering," I would later learn.

"This looks pretty cool, don't you think?" Mo asked.

"Totally," I said.

Of course, it looked pretty cool to the two of us, I thought; something new and different on the spiritual path that neither of us had yet explored. What could possibly be cooler?

We delved into the details of Ama's visit, the when and where of it, having decided right then and there to go to the *Satsang* together if our schedules allowed. Ama was to be in the Santa Fe area the following weekend.

According to the flyer, Ama had established several ashrams, Hindu places of worship, throughout the country. In addition, Ama had devoted her life to helping the poor and had established orphanages and schools, mainly in India.

Ama traveled around the world on a regular basis holding *Satsangs* and, strangely enough was referred to as the "hugging saint," because when she blessed the attendees, she did so with an actual hug.

People would line up for an hour or more after Ama's talks to get hugged by her, this round lady in an orange sari, with long dark thick hair down to her waist and a red dot in the middle of her forehead, called a bindi.

Okay, I thought, I was going to learn something about Hinduism here in the Southwestern United States by meeting a traveling Hindu saint. At this point in time, I had had virtually no exposure to Eastern religions at all. While not really New Agey, Eastern religions, to me, conjured up images of the Beatles meeting up with Indian Gurus and learning to meditate in the Sixties.

While Christianity and Judaism were familiar to me, Hinduism was new, exotic, exciting and decidedly different. If the Beatles could dabble with Eastern religions, why couldn't Mo and I?

I hoped to receive a blessing for my upcoming decision and maybe a hug. Mo was simply curious. Ever the seeker, she was checking out whoever and whatever struck her fancy in the world of Santa Fe healers.

In all honesty, I was growing weary of the constant spiritual search I had been on for the past seven years. If nothing else, the numerous healers I had met had taught me that life is actually for living. In some ways, I had been thinking a lot about living without actually doing it. I was ready to jump and immerse myself in the real thing: life, rather than continually analyzing it. To me this meant leaving the cocoon of Santa Fe behind and flying out into the big wide world to test my new wings.

Mo had no idea that I was seriously thinking about moving. Thus far, Emmy and Nellie hadn't been overly supportive of my decision. I wondered if Mo would behave differently when I broke the news to her.

I was worried she might feel I was rejecting her lifestyle or, worse still, that I was abandoning her. Mo struck me as someone who would be in Santa Fe for the rest of her life.

Mo was older than me. She was in her early fifties and had already lived an entire life and had a full career before moving to Santa Fe. Once she'd made the break from all those ties, I didn't think she'd ever go back to a traditional lifestyle again.

We finished our coffee, got up from the table, and headed for the door of the Lighthouse.

"Have a good week," Mo said.

"You too."

"See ya."

We hugged lightly and went our separate ways.

I smiled to myself as I contemplated the upcoming meeting with Ama. I just had a good feeling about meeting her, based on the radiance that emanated from her photograph.

In the ensuing week, I went about my work life as usual. My job at the book publishing company had afforded the luxury of meeting several famous personalities, including Frank Waters, who wrote *Book of the Hopi*, and artist R. C. Gorman, a Navajo artist who was renowned for his paintings of Native American women. However, most days I spent my time laying out text on the computer and inputting changes from editors and proofreaders prior to final publication.

I worked in a guesthouse that had been converted into an office situated behind my employers' home. My office mates were the husband-and-wife team who owned the company, as well as a full-time editor and an administrative assistant. My hours were 10 a.m. to 6 p.m. and the dress code was casual.

Only in Santa Fe could such an arrangement exist, I thought. In spite of the quirkiness of my job, we churned out high-quality, well-received books and we all worked hard.

As the weekend approached, I started getting excited about going to see Ama. It was a beautiful Saturday evening in early spring when Mo and I met up to head to the *Satsang*. She came to pick me up and seemed smiling and bubbly when I opened the door of my apartment.

"You and me, Sara," she said. "Always up for an adventure."

"Yup, adventure buddies," I said grinning.

We left right away. Mo drove south of town as the glowing evening sun floated just above the horizon, causing us to squint the whole way there. We followed directions that I had written down from the flyer.

We wound through the back roads, which soon turned to dirt. We stopped at a fork and were signaled by brightly colored flags that I later learned were Buddhist prayer flags. A hand-written sign with an arrow on it said: "This Way to Amachi Satsang." We followed the sign, both literally and figuratively.

Even though I had made the rounds of spiritual teachers, I was not yet done with my exploration; the flyer in the bookstore had been a sign. I was now on my way to something new again, feeling open-minded and curious; the way one would feel if one were visiting a foreign country for the first time.

We made small talk on the ride out of town. I was feeling chatty and light-hearted. I was happy to be with my buddy Mo, sampling another bite of the local spiritual fare. The opportunities for personal growth were abundant and it had become more of a fun, rather than deadly serious pasttime for me to continually check out healers and gurus who passed through.

I recalled then Mo telling me the story of how she had packed up and left Boston with everything she owned in her car. Stripped down to life's essentials, Mo had moved to Santa Fe. No sooner had she arrived in town than she was involved in a car accident in which her Oldsmobile was totaled.

"It was too heavy for my new life," Mo had said.

She and I had always had a special connection. Maybe Mo's big black car was kind of like my deadbeat husband—too heavy for my new life—energetically speaking. Like Mo and her car, I just didn't need to cart around all that baggage anymore.

I thought about telling Mo about my impending move. At this point I was pretty sure I was going to Denver. I had been kicking it around for a while and I figured, if I got accepted, I would go.

I didn't have a chance to, though, because it took most of our joint energy to navigate the dirt roads and to get to the *Satsang*'s location. I would tackle that on the way home afterwards, I thought. Plus, I was reluctant to do it before the event. It could potentially ruin the day.

As we pulled up to the *Satsang*, I saw a main house, a couple guesthouses and then a large open field with an enormous white tent right in the middle. As it turned out, a wealthy couple from Los Angeles hosted Ama every year on their land, a vast plot of arid desert.

We parked. Not knowing at all what to expect, we got out of the car along with throngs of people who crowded the makeshift lot. We all started walking through the dust toward the tent. It was twilight. I was awaiting a hug from the Divine Mother.

I took a deep breath and grabbed Mo as we took our place in line, joining a lengthy procession that snaked loosely through the private estate.

I began to feel chilled as my sun-drenched skin cooled down in the approaching evening. I trembled slightly with fear, or was it excitement? Would this mysterious saint give me the validation I was seeking for my choice to leave Santa Fe?

I desperately wanted some reassurance that I was doing the right thing. After all, moving was a big deal; uprooting oneself from routine, home, friends, work, and a community that had nurtured me. I had finally felt settled.

But I feared I was at a dead-end in Santa Fe. Settled meant living hand-to-mouth on the fringes of society, never plugging back into the mainstream. Maybe I was bored with all the self-seeking I had been doing. Maybe I was just ready for a change.

Maybe instead of constantly seeking, I could actually just arrive at my destination, spiritually speaking. And then just live my life integrating spirituality into my day-to-day reality. What a concept.

Finally, we reached the massive white tent and, after a short wait in line, were shown inside, seated in the middle toward the back. We were packed tightly into the tent, but no one was pushing or shoving. I felt a little claustrophobic. I told myself it was a friendly, peaceful group. Many were seated in silent meditation with their eyes closed. No one was speaking.

I looked around briefly, noticing the usual suspects that seemed to populate most of these events I had been attending in and around Santa Fe. There were aging hippies, reclusive rock stars, and Hollywood actors on hiatus from paparazzi. I saw young people like myself who were basically curious about what was going on and I saw New Age wannabes, decked out in newly purchased crystal or Native American jewelry that screamed out, I am hip and cool, and I am hanging out in Santa Fe.

In spite of my categorizing people, the all-pervasive stillness that permeated the space around me helped me to relax.

Far away, at the front of the tent, a makeshift stage was set up. Up front were a dozen or more devotees, most of whom looked to be from India and were dressed in flowing white cotton.

The entourage swarmed the stage as the tent filled to capacity. Finally, an Indian man dressed all in white spoke to the crowd through a microphone. He welcomed us and then said he would translate for Ama, who didn't speak English.

Then I saw a little round woman walk onto the stage and sit down at the front with no fanfare. At first, I wasn't sure it if it was her, because she was so unassuming. Ama too was dressed in white and had a bindi in the middle of her forehead. She began to chant and everyone in the audience closed their eyes.

Ama and her entourage sang in an undulating rhythm, swaying methodically as if in a trance. The words were called a mantra, I learned. The mantra is designed to help in meditation by providing a focus for the mind. Soothing words repeated over and over slowly calm the nervous system and help racing thoughts slow down.

Ama then spoke briefly through the translator about her work in India supporting the poor, starting schools and orphanages all over the country and then the world. She spoke of her spiritual awakening at a young age and how, even as a girl, she was sought after and proclaimed a saint. She was from a poor family somewhere in a tiny village in India. I felt highly inspired because it was mainly due to her good works and her desire to serve that she became known.

She said her devotees would perform a blessing ceremony for us, called a *puja*. We were to relax and enjoy the sound of the chanting, letting it carry us far away.

Then members of Ama's entourage brought out small platters with candles on them and began to walk down the aisles, while continuing to recite prayers for the audience.

I began to feel dazed and tired. The ceremony was long and confusing. I alternated between peaceful calm and occasional agitation. I was actually sweating. Even though it was night, the body heat in the tent felt stifling. I must have drifted off into a deep meditative state, however because, at a later point, I was jolted into consciousness as though awakening from a deep sleep.

As the swamis were walking up and down with their little platters with candles, the crowd began chanting to Ama's lead.

I breathed in the sweet incense all around me and began to focus my awareness within.

I felt a deep stillness settle upon me. It was as though all my life I had been running toward something or away from something and suddenly I just stopped.

My thoughts slowed way down, until it seemed like I experienced only an awareness of my breath: In and out, in and out. I was an aware, conscious being, in a body, breathing, in a room with other aware, conscious beings in bodies that were also breathing.

There was nowhere I needed to be. There was nothing I needed to do. Just be here now, I thought. And it was truly blissful just to let everything go.

Eventually the ceremony ended, and we were directed into several long lines to await the personal hug that was offered to all in attendance.

I looked at Mo. She seemed like she was sleepwalking. She seemed totally out of it and was not speaking. While Mo appeared trancelike, I realized she was simply inwardly focused.

"Are you up for this?" I whispered.

She nodded affirmatively but still didn't speak.

We meandered into a line in the center of the room. Ama's staff members were monitoring the flow of people and making sure the crowd was orderly and alternating appropriately between the three lines. Ama was seated on several cushions in the center of the stage. One by one, people knelt down before her and received an embrace.

As I stood there and looked at this woman known as the Divine Mother who was smiling and hugging hundreds of individuals, I was struck by her absolute humbleness. Ama was completely unassuming. In fact, I imagined if I were walking down a street in a village in India and I saw her, she would look perfectly ordinary.

Ama showed me that one could be an ordinary person and still lead an extraordinary life. I thought of the millions of children living in squalid conditions in Third World countries that she had helped. I imagined the poverty she had seen all around her growing up and yet, there she was, surrounded by wealthy Westerners who wanted something from her—that unnamable, yet constantly sought-after inner peace that seems to elude so many—which money and worldliness cannot provide.

After about twenty minutes, we were next in line. I motioned Mo to go ahead of me. She stepped forward and knelt down in front of Ama. I watched as Mo was rocked in Ama's arms for a brief moment then released. I saw her stand up and observed her waiting for me on the other side of Ama. I couldn't read her expression. The tent was dimly lit and smoky from incense and candles.

Then it was my turn. A member of Ama's staff motioned for me to step forward and get my hug. I did as I had seen others do before me, knelt down in front of Ama and felt a bear-like embrace. Suddenly Ama muttered something deep and guttural in my ear, pulled me close to her and released me. A staff member helped me to my feet and motioned me to move on.

I was dizzy and all the blood had drained from my face. I felt a little sick and at the same time a little silly. Intense waves of emotion began to wash over me. Unable to move, I stood still, frozen in space.

I realized that I now looked like most of the others I had seen after they had received their hug: deer in the headlights, zoned out, reeling from something powerful yet incomprehensible. What force that woman gave out with her touch. I forgot momentarily that I had gone to the *Satsang* seeking validation. I was simply caught up in the moment.

Once I got my bearings a little bit and the waves had begun to subside, I realized there would be no way to ever know what Ama had whispered in my ear. It was obviously some sort of a prayer or blessing.

In an instant I felt cheated, ripped off. How was I to

interpret her mumblings? What did it all mean? I wanted to have something definitive happen. Now, here it was and there was nothing solid coming from the experience that I could hang onto.

I swayed in dismay. Then I opened my eyes and came to. There I was in the tent with all these seekers wanting answers. A sense of ridiculousness overtook me and I almost laughed out loud. I understood then that I needed to let my answer come from within. No one or nothing outside of me could provide it.

This is what the experience of meeting Ama was all about: I was high—I was low-—I was happy—I was depressed—I was angry—I was at peace—and it was all happening in the span of a nanosecond. It was unfathomable.

Suddenly Mo was beside me, waving her hand in front of my face.

"Sara, you all right there?" she asked, grinning.

"Oh, man, I guess so," I said.

"Come on," she said, motioning me toward the door. "Let's get some air."

And out we walked into a starlit night. The sky was deep blue and fabulous. The stars were a million pinpricks of light. Mo started the car and we pulled out of the parking lot, following a line of headlights as we moved in slow motion onto the highway.

Both of us were quiet, blissed-out, in our separate spaces. But it was okay. There was nothing to say. We were simply hanging out together in silence.

I realized then that whether Mo did or didn't support my decision to leave Santa Fe, I would be fine.

Part of my journey to Santa Fe in the first place had

been about learning to trust myself, my own unique path, and the twists and turns that were part of it that were mine and mine alone.

I knew deep within myself as we drove home in perfect, peaceful silence that I would be leaving soon. It just felt right. It actually didn't matter what Ama had said to me. I silently blessed myself in this next phase of my life.

SHEDDING THE PAST

Each of us has an inner room where we can visit to be cleansed of fear-based thoughts and feelings. This room, the holy of holies, is a sanctuary of light.

~ Marianne Williamson

A couple of weeks after the *Satsang*, I got a letter in the mail from the University of Denver. I sat in my apartment alone and opened it with trembling hands. I scanned it quickly, afraid of what it might say. I hadn't applied to any other schools. This was it. I was either going or I wasn't. I had no other options.

I breathed a huge sigh of relief: it was an acceptance letter for the Master of Communication program for the coming fall. Actually, classes would begin the last week of August, it said. My life had opened up and a new direction had presented itself.

I kept thinking I had to tell Mo. I'd postponed it once already. She was really the last one of my friends who needed to know. I wasn't so much asking their permission, as I was being truthful to those to whom I had gotten close, my Santa Fe family. Holding back any longer from Mo seemed to me like telling a lie by omission.

It was hard that Nellie and Emmy hadn't understood why I wanted to leave Santa Fe. I didn't want to alienate anyone; especially those who had stood by me when I had been really struggling. That wasn't my intention. But I needed at least one person to continue their support now.

With trepidation, I called Mo.

"Hey there," I said when Mo answered. "I've got some awesome news."

"Cool. I'm dying to hear."

"Well, um," I said haltingly. "I'm so happy. I got accepted to the University of Denver's Communication Department. I start in August."

"Congratulations, you little shit," Mo said affectionately. "I knew you had something up your sleeve the day of the *Satsang*. I was just biding my time waiting to hear what it was."

"Really?" I said.

"You bet. I'm so happy for you."

I breathed a sigh of relief; my second, deep sigh that morning. Mo was not going to question my decision. In fact, she seemed supportive. Mo had actually understood. She had totally gotten it about my desire to make a change.

"Thanks," I said.

"I'll miss you, of course, Sara," Mo said. "But, let's face it, you're not gonna be here for your whole life."

"I'm not? What'd ya mean?"

"I've seen it here before, that's all. Folks get their fill of all the woo woo stuff going on and then they're ready to test their spiritual chops out in the real world—see how their inner growth has actually served them."

"Yup. That about sums it up," I said.

Then Mo and I talked about the actual nuts and bolts of my move. She referred me to a friend of hers who was looking to make some extra cash and who might be able to drive a U-Haul up to Colorado for me when the time came.

Yikes. This was suddenly all too real. I did not give my notice at work that week but thought long and hard about it, knowing this step was coming up soon. Everything looked different all of a sudden as I viewed the details of my day-to-day life, knowing they would all change in a few short months. My job, my co-workers, the quaint little guesthouse that had been my office for the past few years would all soon become just memories.

In essence, I would be leaving the safety of the known. I was making a shift from spiritual to professional. Knowing I would soon be Denver-bound, I took it upon myself to see a couple more sights on my own before I left.

The Santuario de Chimayo, a 400-year-old Spanish Catholic church, was one of my final day trips. I decided to go the following weekend after my talk with Mo. Even though it was considered a tourist attraction, it would be a shame for me to leave the area without having seen it.

Time was of the essence, since I was moving in a few months. After all, it was mid-March and classes were starting the last week of August. I counted the months aloud to myself. April, May, June, July, August. Yikes, I had just five months to get it together to move.

The Santuario was built on top of a sacred site that had been revered by the Native Americans for centuries prior to the Spanish settlement in northern New Mexico. Going back hundreds of years, the dirt at the site was rumored to have healing properties. It was said to have contributed to spontaneous healings if rubbed on one's ailment.

I had wanted to see the Santuario de Chimayo for some time. I made the decision to go alone to have some time to reflect on the changes that were coming up for me. I also wanted to think about where I had been.

I had been in Santa Fe exactly seven years. The number seven was a symbol of completion. Christians considered the seven to be sacred, i.e. God created the earth in six days and rested on the seventh. While I almost never thought of Christianity in relation to my own life, this seemed like more than just mere coincidence, especially since I was on my way to visit a historic church.

I realized I was finally in a good place emotionally and spiritually. What a long haul it had been since I had arrived in Santa Fe, clutching at an unfulfilling relationship to make me whole. Once Michael was pried out of my clenched fists by some cosmic force, I had begun the slow process of filling myself up.

I drove out of town on a Saturday morning. By this time, I was accustomed to the scrub oak-covered rolling hillsides and the wide vistas that appeared as soon as I left the city limits. Although familiar, I never tired of the stark beauty of the land surrounding Santa Fe. I was going to miss the landscape.

The lure of Santa Fe and its environs had played out in the lives of others long before my time. Painter Georgia O'Keefe and photographer Ansel Adams found the sparse landscape to be mystical and creatively stimulating. So too did writers Willa Cather and D. H. Lawrence. Maybe the concept of sacred geography, the pinpointing of geographic locations as sacred places, was more universal than I had known at the time.

Before long, I had arrived in Chimayo, a town built before the automobile was invented. Ristras adorned the tightly knit cluster of homes and shops crowding the narrow main street. I waited my turn in the slow, single lane of traffic that curved through the town of Chimayo, anticipating my visit to the Santuario.

On the way to the Santuario, I was feeling exhilarated. I had been eager to learn what I could from the place and the day. I hoped would be able take the experience with me somehow into the new life that awaited me in Denver.

I reached the Santuario parking lot and pulled in among the other cars. An arroyo (dried riverbed) snaked its way toward the Santuario from the parking area along the road. I walked along it, following the other pilgrims to the church.

It seemed odd to me to be a tourist in my own backyard. There I was visiting a local historic landmark alongside heavy German-speaking sightseers with big cameras and Texans wearing cowboy hats and speaking with a loud twang. I traveled light: shorts, backpack, water bottle, sunglasses, and Tevas to walk in, of course.

When I arrived at the church, I saw an old, small, building that looked more dilapidated than I would have imagined for a historic landmark. I felt slightly disappointed as I wondered why it hadn't been better maintained. It was a picture of austerity amid the pinon trees on the banks of a dried-up tributary.

Standing at the entrance, I could see nothing of the Pueblo that had once existed on the site of the Santuario. As odd as it seemed, it was actually a common practice for the Spaniards to build churches adjacent to Native American Pueblos and other sites. Each of the seven major Pueblos that encircled Santa Fe also had small Catholic churches on their grounds.

The church is traditional, rigid, patriarchal, hierarchical and so unlike the Native Americans and their legitimate connection to the land. And, if it was the earth itself that already had the healing properties then why build a structure, in this case a place of worship, on top of it?

This situation—of the church coopting something from another culture that already existed—was reminiscent of other Santa Fe paradoxes I had already witnessed: the rich white baby boomers seeking solace from a poor Indian saint; the popularity of Native American jewelry and pottery, yet the lifestyle of the Native Americans themselves not enhanced by this trend. The ancient Chinese healing art of acupuncture had become all the rage in Santa Fe, a small town in the Southwestern U.S. And on and on it went. The City Different was filled with ironies.

This theme of holy ground had been following me since I had first done the vision quest at Nellie's directive. It was during my dream that I had been strongly drawn to Santa Fe—the land specifically. It was largely due to the special vibe of Santa Fe itself that had allowed my spiritual journey to unfold.

I walked into the church and began to look around. I wanted to get a sense of the basic and deep-seated healing vibrations that had impacted so many throughout history. The main chamber of the Santuario was quaint but common, filled with pews, candles, and a basic but beautiful altar.

Adjacent to the worship area was a cramped and tiny alcove, crowded with written testimonials. I walked toward it. The small area was jammed with curiosity seekers and the room was dim. I saw several pairs of discarded crutches with letters pinned to them with messages like, "after visiting the Santuario de Chimayo and rubbing its healing dirt on my leg, I was able to walk again and no longer needed my crutches..."

Trinkets of all sizes, shapes and colors littered the room, dolls with cotton dresses and tiny frozen faces, faded ribbons, coins from various countries. Strewn around in every direction were bouquets of dried flowers, handwritten notes taped to every inch of wall space, figurines, and personal offerings, both lavish and simple.

Along the far end of the room was a gaping hole in the floor where the healing clay was accessible. People crowded toward it, kneeling down and scooping up handfuls of the sacred dirt and putting it into little vials to take home with them. Some cried openly; some somberly rubbed the dirt between their palms, whispering prayers.

In addition to the usual roundup of tourists, surprisingly, I bumped into a number of local Latinos among the visitors. Some were praying solemnly.

Then it struck me that this place, while a historic and tourist attraction, was still a house of worship. While no clergy members were active there, it was obvious that the locals considered the Santuario a holy place. In fact, I had learned from literature at the entrance that each year during Holy Week, the week before Easter, hundreds of devout walkers from nearby towns converge on the Santuario de Chimayo to remember departed loved ones and give thanks for the miracles that occurred there.

I waited my turn to approach the hole with the sacred dirt, feeling a strange solemnity. I knelt down and touched the clay-like powder. The dirt was dry, like the New Mexican soil and brown like the adobe walls of the Santuario. It was light and porous and smelled of rain. I said a prayer, asking for my own healing, while holding some dirt, and then I let it go, and watched as it silently slid through my fingers.

I wondered if the effects would be nullified if I washed my hands. I wondered too if the Santuario would ever run out of healing dirt if everyone who came through its doors for hundreds of years took a little bit home with them in a container.

I stood up, but I didn't take any with me. The spirituality of this place could not actually be contained in a vial, I realized. The lessons I had learned in Santa Fe were portable, not confined to a place. The dirt is a symbol of the land I had been drawn to and, while I would soon be leaving this locale, my spirituality would travel with me. So, it was not the physical dirt that I would be taking with me. It was something else that was already within.

With a sense of accomplishment, I moved back through the line of people waiting for their turn to scoop up a tiny sample of the special dirt to take home with them. I saw the place with a new perspective. The Santuario was a place where those who entered could lay down their burdens, seek and receive tangible divine assistance, become light rather than heavy, empowered rather than powerless.

I left the church and walked outside into the bright sunlight. I felt peaceful. While I didn't understand what spontaneous healing meant or know whether or not I believed in it at all, I had been deeply moved by the testimonials I had witnessed inside.

In my own life, I had sought the same kind of relief. I had come to Santa Fe seeking clarity, a new direction, a greater ability to give and receive love.

While I too had experienced great healing from my time there, I had begun to regard Santa Fe as more of a state of mind rather than a place.

I felt more attentive than usual as I walked along the arroyo and back to my car. I felt a slight breeze rustle my hair and noticed that the needles of the pinon trees bowed and swayed slightly too. Clouds overhead responded to the wind, moving and swirling.

For an instant, I felt an unusual kinship to the others who had passed before me on this land. I felt connected to the land, the Spanish Catholics worshipping at the Santuario 300 years ago and to the Native Americans who held healing ceremonies on the same spot 1,000 years before that. I felt attuned to myself and the inner knowing that had brought me here to experience a deep, timeless wisdom.

As I approached my car in the parking lot, I decided to keep going a little farther and take a walk, following the arroyo as it meandered dustily at the feet of tall swaying cottonwoods.

I walked for a little way, making sure I was actually following the riverbed so I wouldn't get lost. My sense of direction had always been lacking. In Santa Fe, since I sometimes hiked alone, I learned to compensate for it by checking for landmarks sometimes two or three times in the course of half an hour, so I would be able to find my way back in the direction I had come.

Strangely enough, I was more concerned with getting lost than I was with being attacked by either a wild animal, such as a fox or a coyote, or even a depraved human being. Hiking around Santa Fe seemed friendly to me. I ran into people (solo or in groups), who usually said hello and kept right on going.

The sun was strong in the heat of the day. I took a swig of water and applied some sunscreen. I pulled on my pink baseball cap (my hiking hat) and set off walking along the sandy riverbed.

Getting my bearings, I looked around and then for some unknown reason, out of impulse or through a lucky happenstance, I looked down. Lying close to my feet was a fully formed snakeskin. It looked like that the snake—probably a rattler—had just slithered out moments before.

I looked around to see if that was, in fact, the case. I didn't want to stumble onto a rattlesnake, although I'd heard of others meeting up with snakes on hikes in this part of the country and it was rumored that they were more afraid of us than we were of them. Still, I didn't want to find out.

Not seeing or hearing anything ominous, I bent down to take a look. The snakeskin was fully intact. It seemed to be about a foot long. It was dry and looked like fish scales woven together. I touched it with a stick and detected no movement. I bent down and touched it with my fingertips. It felt like parchment.

I picked it up. It weighed almost nothing. I held it up to look at the full length of it in front of me. It spoke to me personally of transformation. I took it to be a sign.

Right then and there, I decided to give myself permission to interpret messages on my own without an intermediary. If my experiences in Santa Fe had given me nothing else, at least they had given me the right to spiritual independence.

I remembered from reading Jamie's book *Animal Spirit Cards* that shedding skin is a symbol of rejuvenation and new life. I also knew from living in Santa Fe that snakes and other reptiles, like lizards, periodically shed their skin. The old skin has to be shed before the new one can grow.

A quote from Joseph Campbell came to me then. It was something like, "We must be willing to let go of the life we planned, in order to have the life that is waiting for us."

I was starting to sweat in the heat. I took a big gulp of water from my water bottle. The snakeskin was all about my upcoming new life in Denver, I decided. I, like the snake that had recently vacated its skin, had changed. I had let go of the life I planned to live and was living differently, more authentically, experiencing the richness of the unknown.

I left the snakeskin there. I didn't need to take that with me either. I turned around empty-handed and began walking back to my car. In addition to feeling overheated, I was getting hungry. It was past lunchtime, so I picked up my pace.

As had become my routine, I used my solitary hikes as time to think. I had been seriously thinking about changing my name before I moved to Denver. The snakeskin made me think about it again.

Sure, Santa Fe was likely the name-change capital of the country. Everybody was doing it: Sanskrit names, new age-y names, nature names, I had known so many people who had changed their names for one reason or another, maybe just because they could.

I didn't think I would actually do it myself. Yet, here I was seriously contemplating it, for real. I liked my first name okay, but it seemed too plain. My last name seemed too short. I had always wanted a longer, more colorful name. Something that flowed, something that felt like mine.

The symbolism of taking on a new name was attractive to me; it meant taking on a new identity. Many traditions had rites of passage for young people moving from childhood into adulthood, often associated with the taking on of a new name.

I too had undergone a rite of passage, becoming transformed over a seven-year period. From a rigid upbringing in New England that had left me spiritually bankrupt, I had somehow landed in a seekers paradise where could and did explore numerous spiritual paths. I had embraced a little bit of each one of them until I had crafted a spirituality that worked for me. Like a patchwork quilt, my spiritual life had been pieced together to form an elaborate whole.

It seemed only fitting that I give myself a new name to acknowledge the change I had undergone. I had been toying with the idea of giving myself a new middle and last name and then keeping Sara as my first name, but using the middle name, when I got to Denver. I had always liked the name Mariah and it felt a little weightier than Sara, more substantial. It was also prettier and more feminine. Sara had always seemed too plain for my personality. I once had a friend with the last name of Rose, and I had always liked that too.

As I walked back toward my car along the arroyo, I thought to myself, I *am* like a rose. I can be sweet, but I also have thorns. If you are don't approach me carefully, you're likely to prick your finger and recoil. You'll definitely be more careful the next time. Okay, I am overly sensitive and somewhat defensive. But once I let you get close to me, I am loyal to a fault.

Finally, I got to my car, opened the door to let it cool off a minute, and collapsed into the driver's seat. My water was gone. In spite of my dehydrated state, the name rang true.

Mariah Rose, I thought. Yes. Mariah Rose is who I have become. My name is Sara Mariah Rose.

All of the inward reflection I had done had finally morphed into a whole new identity, with a new name to match.

How will I ever explain this to my poor parents? I asked myself, half laughing. But changing my name was just one more thing I had to do.

Like the snake who had shed its entire skin, like the cripples who had thrown down their crutches and walked again, I was blossoming into someone new.

TIMELESS DANCE

He who would learn to fly one day must first learn to stand and
walk and run and climb and dance; one cannot fly into flying.

~ Friedrich Nietzsche

I called Nellie to say goodbye. I was sitting in my
apartment surrounded by half-filled cardboard moving
boxes. Piles of clothes, household items, and miscellaneous
trappings of my life lay strewn about.

I wanted to have some closure with Nellie. I wanted to
tell her how much she'd meant to me for the past seven
years. She'd been my rock, my compass, and my sounding
board. Shit, I was really going to miss her.

In spite of my attachment to Nellie and my genuine
love for her, our relationship was actually quite
complicated. I mulled it over while I made piles of stuff in
my living room: stuff that was coming with me, stuff that
was going to Goodwill, stuff to throw away.

The mechanical nature of my task gave me the mental
space I needed to contemplate the enigma that was Nellie.

Let's face it, Nellie had been a surrogate mother for me
all these years. I had left home young and, although I had
a mother, she was far away geographically. Besides, my
own mother had not been supportive my spiritual search.
She had more traditional goals for me and was

embarrassed by my 'years trying to find myself.' So, Nellie was the mother I had always wanted, up to a point. And then I had moved on from her too, as though I were leaving home all over again.

I knew Nellie was pretty attached to being my spiritual navigator and self-appointed mentor. While I had gone along with it for many years, I was growing tired of our dynamic. Nellie was my teacher; I was her student. She was wise and I was naïve. Nellie had truly been my guide for me for a number of years, but I had reached the point where I didn't need her in that way anymore.

This had happened gradually. I couldn't remember a tipping point. But slowly, as I had gained confidence in myself, I started to trust my own inner guidance more and more.

Nellie and I had never quite been on equal footing to begin with. I always placed Nellie on a pedestal, thinking that she knew what was right for me more than I did for myself. I hadn't trusted myself totally when I had first moved to Santa Fe. But that had all changed for me. Since I was leaving town, it was nearing the end of that phase for both of us. I had taken my power back and here I was, all of a sudden, calling my own shots.

Nellie and I had slowly stopped hanging out as much as we used to during my last couple of years in Santa Fe. It hadn't been deliberate on either of our parts. The separation between us just had evolved over time. But thinking about her that day made me realize that there had been a blatant shift. Nellie did not like the fact that I no longer hung on her every word.

I hadn't consulted her about my decision to go to grad school in Denver. When I had told her about my decision, she had given me a disapproving look, and then she was very quiet. I was moving on. Nellie was being edged out of my life and she wasn't happy about it at all. I can't say that I blamed her.

Nellie was actually having a harder time letting go than I was. I could only guess that the power shift in our relationship also was difficult for her to swallow. Nellie had definitely been a spiritual leader; someone who had influenced me greatly and for whom I'd had a great deal of respect. Not to mention the fact that I'd trusted her guidance fully. But, when you're on a spiritual journey, although you meet all sorts of guides, eventually you have to leave them behind and walk alone. For me that time had come.

I dialed the phone. Nellie picked up on the first ring.

We exchanged hellos but Nellie cut right to the chase. I had to hand it to her. Nellie never missed a beat. She was keenly aware that I was leaving town and wanted to make sure to make one last point.

"There's one more spiritual thing you need to do, Sara," Nellie said. "You've gotta attend the annual Corn Dance at one of the Pueblos."

"You mean Mariah," I said, surprised to find myself irritated all of a sudden. "I'm so over all this spiritual stuff."

"Sara," Nellie said, emphasizing my name as she knew it. "This is important. I realize you're busy right now, but trust me, you won't regret this."

Nellie had stubbornly refused to use my new name. When I had told her several weeks earlier about my decision to change my name, I figured she'd be happy, but she had simply not acknowledged it.

I assumed she was mad because I'd decided to change my name without letting her in on it until it was a done deal. In other words, I hadn't asked for her permission, which in Nellie's world meant I had disrespected her.

For a moment, I was tempted just to tell her no. But Nellie had not led me astray before. She had always been spot-on with her recommendations. I knew I could trust her even if she was a royal pain sometimes. "Okay, I'll go," I said at length.

I had been thinking about visiting one of the Pueblos before I moved away. Just like the Santuario de Chimayo, it was a tourist attraction that I had saved until the very end of my stay.

Going to a dance was better than just walking around. This was a chance to see a real Indian ceremony. It seemed fitting that I do it and also that I follow Nellie's guidance one more time.

After all, she knew her shit and had proven it to me time and time again. Even though I felt 'finished' with Santa Fe and was ready to get on with my new life in Denver, I wanted to make sure I wasn't being impatient.

I had ultimately agreed to go because I hoped the experience would prove personally meaningful and would add to my understanding of my own spiritual path.

If Nellie said I needed to see the Corn Dance, then so be it. I would listen to her. But I wanted her to come along not only as a friend but as a mentor. I didn't feel like spending one of my last days in Santa Fe alone and if I was to go with someone, I wanted to be Nellie. She would be the most knowledgeable about the Dance. Besides I wanted to say goodbye.

"I need you to come with me. It will help to have someone to drive with. I'm not up for doing anything that will take up all my energy over a weekend since I'm trying to pack."

There was silence on her end. "I'd like to go with you, but I've already seen the Corn Dances," she said, sounding unenthusiastic. "Plus, it's so dang hot at the Pueblo this time of year."

"Nellie," I said, pleadingly. "This is likely going to be the last time we get to do something together 'til who knows when. I'm moving, remember?

"And you can call me Sara the whole day," I added after a beat.

"Okay. I'll come with you to the Corn Dance," Nellie said after a prolonged silence.

I didn't ask her why she suddenly obliged and she didn't volunteer.

"Thanks so much," I said.

I was sincere. Although there was new tension between us, I was still looking forward to spending time with Nellie for purely sentimental reasons and happy that she would accompany me to the Pueblo.

We decided on the Pueblo of Santo Domingo, August 4, for the annual Corn Dance. My departure date was less than two weeks after that, August 15.

The Santo Domingo Pueblo is midway between Albuquerque and Santa Fe, about five minutes off Highway 25. Santo Domingo is not an obscure village. Tourists were welcomed spectators at these dances. The dance was to be performed by the Tewa tribe, who inhabited Santo Domingo Pueblo. Additionally, as I would discover, it was a multi-cultural festival.

The Corn Dances are common to the nineteen Pueblos that line a northern tributary of the Rio Grande from Isleta in the south to Taos in the north. Their dates come at intervals between May and September, but the largest number occurs regularly in August. The Corn Dance celebrates the beginning of the yearly corn harvest.

On the appointed day, we met to drive to the Pueblo. Nellie and I didn't talk much on the way to the Pueblo. Nellie was unusually quiet and whenever we did talk, she made no mention of my name change—she continued to call me Sara the entire day—or the fact that I would soon be leaving. She never brought it up. Denial can be powerful, I figured. But out of respect for Nellie, I let her have her way. I didn't press the name thing, and I didn't belabor the point that I was moving to Denver.

When we arrived at the Pueblo, we parked our car (for a dollar) by a small Ferris wheel and a house of bounce. We were blasted by amplified rock music. Hot dogs, tacos, and cotton candy were for sale. It was much more commercial, like a fair, than I'd expected.

I wondered what the heck was going on. How can this be a spiritual event with so much touristy hoopla? I looked over at Nellie who rolled her eyes. She didn't have to say, I told you so, even though we both knew it was warranted.

Nellie was a purist. She didn't go for these cobbled-together kinds of events with watered-down traditions.

In addition to the carnival, swarms of people were everywhere. Not the tranquil day I had imagined. I looked around the massive gravel lot crammed with local families and tourists.

Native Americans, likely from neighboring Pueblos, also inhabited the open space. Most of the men wore

Western-style shirts, jeans, and cowboy hats, while the women sported turquoise and silver jewelry.

I felt claustrophobic in the oppressive heat. Shit. It was still before noon. This whole scene was a zoo. We couldn't even walk a couple of steps without getting jostled from one side or the other.

It was at this point that I understood why Nellie didn't want to be here. However, I seriously wondered why she was so adamant that *I* attend the Corn Dance. I looked over at her and she was fanning herself with a piece of discarded cardboard. Her entire face, including her expression, was obscured by a large-brimmed straw hat. I didn't need to see it, however, to know what she was thinking. This was going to be a long day, in more ways than one.

We walked toward the central square of the Pueblo and gathered along with hundreds of other spectators in front of a whitewashed church that was built at the edge of the older part of town. The Pueblo was made up of an old section and a newer section. The historic area was composed of a central plaza surrounded by a Spanish-style church.

The only color visible in all directions was mud brown. Traditional Pueblos are built of adobe (clay) slabs with round wooden beams holding up the walls and ceilings. While most of the residents lived in western-style single-family homes, some adobe structures still remained. There was no grass, trees, or shade anywhere in sight. The ground was the same muddy brown color as the buildings. It was hot and dusty.

Around me, men in cowboy hats wiped sweat from their brows with bandanas. Babies cried and women sighed. We were standing in a central plaza. Everyone was waiting for the dance to begin; for the magical moment when the colorful dancers would emerge from the kiva, the round ceremonial mound.

The kiva was about a football field's distance away. Nellie had told me that many Pueblos are constructed this way. The plaza was where the dances would take place. The dancers would emerge from the kiva, costumed and focused, ready to enter into ceremonial dance.

In the distance, I first heard a drumbeat and then a chant of fifty or so men, that sounded halfway between wail and moan. A shiver ran up and down my spine. Wow, I thought, maybe the entire day wouldn't be a waste of time after all.

Then the male dancers appeared, coming toward the crowd in a long line. Some were smeared from head to toe in blue, some in black and white, painted in stripes and circles.

"This is awesome," I said to Nellie as they began to form a large circle right in front of us.

"Shhhh," was all Nellie said.

Geez, Nellie was being so non-communicative. I couldn't connect with her at all. But maybe this was her way of letting me go. Nellie, in spite of her spiritual awareness, was not the most polished communicator I had ever met. I decided not to think about her and just be present with the dancers.

Off to the side of the central plaza, where the dance was happening, was a large contingent of drummers. They drummed and chanted loudly, high and low, loud and soft, in rhythm with something otherworldly. The heat, the crowd, the cotton-candy eating, cranky kids, none of it mattered. I was transfixed. I looked at Nellie, who was completely lost in the dance. Her eyes were wide and unblinking as her body rocked ever so slightly in time with the rhythm of the drumbeat. Maybe she was okay with being here after all.

First the men danced together—all ages—and then a group of women followed. The dancers wore traditional clothing: loincloths for the men, leather dresses with fringe and beaded designs for the women, moccasins, feathers and decorative face and body paint for both. According to a pamphlet I picked up at the entrance, some five hundred dancers would dance that day. It was eleven o'clock in the morning and the dances would continue until sunset.

We hadn't brought folding chairs with us so we had been standing for a couple of hours in the peak of the afternoon heat. As the sun climbed high above us, one group of dancers took a refreshment break, and another took its place.

Women brought out loaves of bread and dishes teeming with hominy and chili. The tables within the adobe houses were open to a family's friends and guests. Families sat on their flat roofs on folding chairs, sheltered beneath umbrellas to watch the tourists and the dancers. I noticed some teenagers hanging out on a back street, cooling off with Cokes and watermelon.

Before I knew it, the afternoon was half gone. And still the dancers kept right on dancing. I was beyond overheated, hungry, and thirsty. The hypnotic rhythm was making me feel spacey.

"I've gotta take a little break," I said to Nellie. She nodded and we moved away from the crowd and dancers.

We walked back toward the carnival and purchased Indian tacos and bottled water from a vendor. Indian taco, I thought, now that's an oddity if there ever was one. An Indian taco is traditional taco mixings: beans, salsa, ground beef, etc., only instead of being served on a tortilla, the ingredients are served atop Indian fry bread, which is really just fried dough.

As I ate my lunch that was a mixture of Native American, Mexican, and Anglo, I was reminded of the conglomeration of cultures in this part of the country. "This is pretty good," I said to Nellie.

"Yup," was all she said. But we grinned and grinned at each other until I couldn't hold it in anymore and I burst out laughing.

Nellie kept it together and didn't laugh out loud. But I could tell she was tickled pink to be there with me. It was a moment of levity in her otherwise hard life. Nellie had three kids by two different men; neither of whom paid child support. I worried about the fact that she was always alone and struggling financially.

She made ends meet while working as a cashier at a health food store. Here was a woman who seemed to have few options. She did odd jobs, nothing really steady or substantial, as she didn't have a profession other than being a Reiki practitioner, which was hardly a way to support a large family singlehandedly.

Maybe she was jealous of me going off and going to graduate school. Who knew?

My friendship with Nellie had had a good run. We both knew that much. And we also both knew that, by the simple fact that I was leaving Santa Fe, our relationship would soon be permanently altered. It was not anyone's fault, I thought. It was just change, just life.

I thought about the many spiritual teachers I had met during my seven years in Santa Fe. All had given me specific gifts. But no one had been more influential than Nellie. She herself had been a gift, steering me in an invisible direction that ultimately had led me to me. Ironically, as I had found myself, I no longer needed Nellie to show me the way.

Like all the spiritual teachers who had come into my life in Santa Fe, Nellie too was leaving it. While I was sad, I was also anxious to get the goodbye over with. I didn't want to drag things out between us. It was hard to part with her, but it was somehow necessary.

We went back to the dance that hadn't stopped during our lunch break. Dancers simply cycled in and out of the main plaza. They sang in mournful tones interwoven with the drumming, locked in step and lost in time. The dances were all circular. A line of dancers would emerge from the kiva onto the plaza and form a huge circle. Then, when each dance was finished, they would leave the plaza in single file. Then another group would come in and do the same thing.

Like Nellie, I too entered a trance-like state where I was no longer thinking about what I was witnessing. I became one with it: the music, chanting, and rhythmic dancers. I didn't feel the heat, dehydration, my sweaty armpits, and aching feet from standing all day. Everything swirled together into a blur where I almost didn't know where my body ended and the dancers began. We became one. I found myself swaying in place to the drumbeats.

I had the profound realization that the Corn Dance I was watching actually was not a show. The dancers were giving thanks for the new harvest of corn and asking for a bountiful crop.

The Tewa were using the symbolic nature of the rhythms, costumes, chants, and drumming to communicate with the earth's spirits. Their whole life and awareness were based on a natural cycle, like the rain dances that are purported to bring life-giving water to keep parched crops from dying. The Pueblo people still danced year-round to communicate their harmony with the earth, the seasons, and their interconnectedness with all that is.

This was their reality and here we were trying to intellectualize what for them was actually just how they lived their lives. For the dancers, spirituality was not merely for ceremony. It was integrated with their daily life. This wasn't drama; it was church.

As I watched the Corn Dance, it seemed like I was actually getting this thing on a deep level. There was a huge contrast between how I'd have perceived this ceremony when I first showed up to Santa Fe and how I was experiencing it that day. If I'd gone to the Corn Dance when I first got to town, it would have been a theatrical experience, just colorful costumes and show. I would have been trying to figure out what was going on by using my mind. But here I was attuned to the subtle nuances of what was happening, not thinking, just feeling the energy of the dance.

True, I was leaving Santa Fe. But I had been steeped in the land, culture, and nuances of the place. I had lived and breathed it for seven years. It had sunk into my bones and become part of me.

My consciousness had slowed down enough and my

mind had opened wide enough for me to take in this level of reality that would have been just beneath the surface of my awareness seven years prior. That day, the meaning of the dance rose up and crashed over me like a wave. I can't really say exactly how or when these realizations hit me. It has something to do with the heat, repetitive movement of the dancers, Nellie refusing to talk (so I had no choice but to just focus on the dances), the mournful wailing of the singers, the incessant drumming, and just the fact that it felt like the dances had been going on forever. They had no beginning and no end.

While I was swaying to the music, I stopped thinking about my own past or my own future. I was just there, in the present with the colors and rhythms, feeling connected to it all on a deep level.

Then, I started thinking about how I was beginning to live my own spirituality, how it was integrated, and not separate from my day-to-day activities. I didn't need to be anywhere or do anything. It was my birthright and I could and would take it with me to Denver.

This thought buoyed me as the dances came to an end at last. It was dark and the crowd, rather than thinning out, grew larger with teenagers who were ready to hit the makeshift carnival. Despite my epiphany, every bone in my body screamed 'go to sleep' as we made our way through the pumped-up crowd of young people coming in and older folks and families leaving.

I wanted to talk to Nellie about my experience of the dance. I wanted to tell her that I was getting it—the deep connection that the Tewa and other tribal peoples had to the land. How they felt themselves to be a part of a greater cosmic whole, not separate from it.

But we drove home without speaking. There was a heaviness between us. Nellie would remain in Santa Fe, her life unchanged. I was moving on to a new life. I had a new name and a new outlook. I was filled up, not empty. I was different than I had been seven years prior.

Nellie, for all intents and purposes, was the same, only older. I began to feel overwhelming compassion for her. Here I was beginning a new cycle while Nellie had plateaued.

Finally, I broke the silence.

"Thanks so much for insisting that I go to the Corn Dance," I said, adding, "And for coming with me."

"You know, Sara," Nellie said, "these dances have been going on long before the white man came, and they'll continue a long time after you and I are both gone."

I never knew what to think of Nellie's cryptic remarks. This was just how she was, I thought. She's going to talk to me about the Tewa people instead of talking about our relationship. But there was no fighting it. And no changing her.

"I know. The dances were really beautiful and moving," I said.

"To the Tewa, they're just a part of daily life. They're not moving at all. It's just what they do."

Okay. Nellie was in one of her moods. Yes. The dances were woven into the lives of these peoples, like making art or music or writing books was woven into our own. And yet, they were more than art. The dances were prayers.

I got to Nellie's house and turned the car off in her driveway. There were no words.

"I can't thank you enough," I said. "For everything."

"You're welcome, Sara," Nellie said. "But right now,

I've gotta see what the kids are up to."

And with that she gave me a short hug and got out of the car.

I sat there for a minute, stunned. Then I turned on the ignition, drove home, and went to bed.

I didn't cry. I didn't even think. I was just bone tired and wanted to sleep. And I did. It was a deep dreamless sleep that fell upon me almost instantly. When I awoke the next day, I was lost in the numerous tasks of moving. I thought of Nellie only fleetingly, but when I did it was with deep fondness.

COMING FULL CIRCLE

You have to lose yourself to find yourself.

~ Willem Dafoe

The day had finally come. It was a crystal-clear morning in late August 1994 when I pulled out of town. My mind was as clear as the day. My heart soared. I breathed deeply. The air was cool in my nostrils. I was beginning a new chapter.

I drove my car crammed with stuff and I was following Johnny, Mo's friend who was driving a U-Haul filled with all my belongings. I wondered how Mo had actually met Johnny. He was a wiry Mexican in his late 20s, I guessed, who looked like he hadn't shaved in a couple of days.

As we hit the highway, Johnny was driving fast—too fast, I thought, for such a heavy load. What the hell, I thought. I kept him in sight as I sped along behind him. I signaled him with my horn and rolled down my window. He looked in the rearview mirror and nodded in acknowledgment as I pointed to a sign to pull off at the next rest stop.

Johnny pulled off the highway at the rest stop. I followed him and we gassed up our respective vehicles, used the restrooms and filled up our travel mugs with mediocre coffee.

I looked over at him and hesitated. "You might want to follow the speed limit," I said. "There may be speed traps set up at the edge of town. Besides that, the load is not all that steady."

I bought some power bars while Johnny decided upon a family-sized bag of Doritos and a king-sized Snickers bar.

Wearing a soiled tee-shirt and baggy jeans, Johnny squinted at me in the store and grunted a thank you as I paid for his grub. That was our deal. I was paying for gas and food, plus a fee for his service; he was driving.

No need to try to make conversation with this guy, I thought. He simply wasn't gonna be a talker. This was actually a good thing. It was a far cry from my relationship with Michael that had so consumed me on the drive to Santa Fe from Boulder seven years prior; This was purely practical, with no strings attached and, it suited me just fine.

We got back on the road pretty quickly. Johnny was going to spend the night in Denver at the apartment I'd secured. He'd sleep on the couch in the living room. And I'd be in the bedroom on a futon. He'd unload the rest of my stuff in the morning and then return the empty U-Haul to Santa Fe.

The drive would be a good place to think. It was a moment of transition and I wanted to savor it before I got busy in my new life in Denver.

I had tried to tie up as many loose ends as possible before I left Santa Fe. Unfortunately, I hadn't been able to wrap things up with Michael in a neat little bow. Much as I had tried, the will to actually see him was simply lacking.

I had started out innocently enough by calling him to say goodbye. However, there was bad blood between us that I hadn't been able to shake off. Less than six months after our break-up, Michael had moved in with the woman he'd been having the affair with.

I had been angrier than I was devastated. After all, Michael was the one who didn't want marriage, didn't want commitment, so he had said. This behavior of his was infuriating at the time, not to mention confusing.

As I continued my spiritual journey though, every once in a while, I would see or hear about Michael. Not surprisingly, things hadn't gone well for him in his new relationship or in his business, either.

He had moved out from the girlfriend after a couple of years and had given up his business to do freelance construction work and odd jobs of the handyman variety.

By the time I was Denver-bound, Michael had been living in a trailer outside of town on someone's barren patch of land. He was broke and directionless.

I had made a couple of half-hearted attempts to call him and try to connect but I was embarrassed and sad for him. I didn't know what to say. Therefore, what had happened was we had simply played phone tag for a few rounds before both of us had given up.

I had left him a message saying I was moving to Denver and he had, in turn, left me one wishing me good luck. So, we had cleared the air between us on a very superficial level, which was how we both chose to leave things. It was for the best, I realized, at least for now.

The drive between Santa Fe and Denver is awesome— it shoots through some of the most beautiful country on the planet. First the endless openness of northern New Mexico; all that land and sky hit me as I headed north on Highway 285 toward Raton Pass.

Then the art galleries and fresh produce stands of Taos. Bright red ristras were hung out to dry, reminding me that I had lived someplace unlike anywhere else in North America. In Taos, there were road signs that read Vaya Con Dios (*Go with God* in Spanish). I couldn't think of any saying more apropos than that was.

Soon Taos was behind us and we were on to Raton Pass. The mountain pass twisted and turned, first climbing, then descending, and curving whether going up or down. As we hit altitude, we drove through a low-hanging thunder cloud and suddenly were pelted by huge raindrops.

By this time, I had passed Johnny. I drove carefully, looking over my shoulder around every switchback to make sure the U-Haul was still on the road. I was afraid Johnny'd take one turn too fast and slide off the embankment, as the truck listed from side to side with every curve.

Out of the drizzle, the sun poked through at the top of the pass. Beyond my wildest dreams, I saw rainbows arching out in every direction; small and large, double, triple, and infinite. The right angle of cloud and afternoon sunrays had produced this miracle, a spectacle to behold.

It had to be a sign.

I had a vision of myself, a little girl called Sara, looking lovingly up into her father's eyes as he tosses her lightly, playfully in the air and catches her, holding her tight as she squeals with laughter.

A mom who brushes little Sara's hair every night, one hundred strokes, she would say, gently coaxing her daughter to count the smooth caress of the brush through her soft brown locks.

A family with siblings—achingly long car trips in the summer, plastered together with sweat and a common bond of genetics.

After kindergarten, came first grade; after elementary school, came junior then senior high. After college, there would be marriage and a career in some city, it was assumed, until the wheels had come off and I landed in New Mexico.

At the time, I had felt like I didn't fit in with my family. I didn't feel like I had met my parents' expectations. And I was certain that there had been something lacking in my upbringing. I had felt alone and disconnected as a child. Yet, it was precisely because I had felt so alienated from any kind of spirituality that I had resisted going down a more conventional path in my late teens and early twenties.

There must have been some sort of divine perfection in my childhood experience of lack that led me to the spiritual questing that I had undertaken in Santa Fe. In this way, my newfound spirituality helped me see my childhood with new eyes.

As a result of being around so many self-identified 'orphans' in Santa Fe, people like me who hadn't fit in with their families of origin, I began to feel more connected to mine. True, I was different. True, I hadn't met their expectations. But, also true, there was mutual love and respect between my parents and me.

In the grand scheme of things, what my parents had wanted for me was to feel good about who I was. They had wanted me to be happy in the way that every parent wants their child to be happy. To be fulfilled, content, joyous, passionate about life. For me to get there, I had to find my own way. They had ultimately surrendered to this fact. And they'd done the hardest thing a parent can ever do and that was to let go.

They let go of the form my life would take and its outward appearance and instead held tightly to the truth of their best dreams for me.

As I moved into the mainstream of life once again, they supported me. And, for the first time in a very long time, I felt their unconditional love.

I thought of my parents then, with a combination of tenderness and respect. I didn't feel the need to defend my lifestyle choice to them or to badger them about perceived lacks in my upbringing. Through all the healing work I'd done, I'd come to a peaceful acceptance about my childhood that felt solid.

Between Anastasia Morningstar's cosmic acupuncture sessions, to communing with the Grandmothers on Suzanne's land at Three Pine Hill, to my women's sweat lodge with Jamie, not to mention my shamanic journey, something had shifted inside me that made room for compassion for the ones who had raised me. After all, weren't they doing the best they could with what they knew to be true at the time? I believed they were.

Now I was back on the straight and narrow, albeit a changed version of myself, better equipped to deal with life's twists and turns. I had been through hell and back, really, in the seven years I had lived in Santa Fe. And, I had actually lived to tell about it, which was no small feat. While there was no guarantee that I wouldn't have my struggles ahead of me in Denver, I felt an inner fullness that buoyed me up. Whereas before I moved to Santa Fe, I had simply felt empty inside.

What a ride it had been. A long, strange trip, I laughed to myself, thinking about the lyrics to that Grateful Dead song. Now here I was coming out the other end of the tunnel and the sun was shining on my future, in spite of the fact that I still had doubts.

Was I doing the right thing in moving to Denver? Would I be okay in a big city? Would the spiritual connection that I'd worked so hard to cultivate carry me through this next big life change or would I get lost in the hustle and bustle again of career and money?

Only time would tell. At that point I was all in and there was no turning back, I thought.

But I was lost again in cloud and sky and highway and sunrays and rainbows and the songs on the radio and the faraway sound of my voice as I sang and laughed and cried and remembered.

I wondered, at the moment of my birth was I destined to this place, this life, these circumstances, this path? Martin, the shaman I had seen several years back, had alluded to the fact that I was at a certain point on my life's journey. He said I was going somewhere but I hadn't arrived yet. Anastasia Morningstar, the acupuncturist, had told me years ago that feeling my pain was an important part of my growth—of claiming my power and of living an authentic life.

So, I had come to understand that some people believe in destiny. Unlike what my parents taught me, that we are all born as blank slates and can simply succeed by pulling ourselves up by our bootstraps if we have a mind to.

I hadn't been raised as any particular religion or been taught about spirituality as a child. And although I had been given everything I could have wanted or needed materially; I had felt the lack of something deeper. I had stability, good schooling, plenty of food to eat, and lots of opportunities to succeed in life, yet I craved a spiritual connection to something that was never even mentioned or acknowledged. Whether that unmentionable was God or the Spirit of the Universe or a Cosmic Force, didn't matter.

This void had led to my spiritual quest, which in turn led to my arrival in Santa Fe seven years prior as a seeker. The mere fact that I wasn't raised in any particular religion made me more open-minded to trying all these different philosophies. It had left the door open to figure it out on my own.

But, had I found what I was looking for? Yes, and no.

There was value in all my one-off spiritual experiences and I'd definitely be carrying that spiritualty with me in my everyday life. I would be able to take pieces of advice I'd received from various people I'd met along the way and apply it to problems I'd inevitably encounter in my new life in Denver.

Did this mean that I would never feel lost again? No. Or, that I'd never again face challenges? Again, no.

In my random, knee-jerk movements from one healer to the next, I had accidentally stumbled upon my spiritual path. I hadn't consciously known what I was doing. But I had known enough to trust my inner guidance and to keep putting one foot in front of the other without understanding where I would end up.

I had 'been led' to various healers, each of who had been like pieces of a puzzle that came together finally to form a whole concept of spirituality that was unique to me.

What it meant to me to be destined to walk a path,

especially one that was challenging, was that I was now walking hand in hand with the universe. In the cosmic sense, I was not alone. There was something greater than me that I was a part of and that I could tap into for sustenance and guidance.

In my day-to-day reality I could ask for guidance at anytime, anywhere. Whether it be on a hike, looking at the sky and paying attention to the birds, in a crowd of people, choosing to feel connected instead of separate: on a city street, in a restaurant, in a car, with my parents. I was a part of something bigger than myself and it was a fact, not something flaky that came and went. It was tangible. It was real.

I had to keep my eyes on the road, I reminded myself. I'm driving. I'm driving. I repeated several times out loud. There were few cars on the road and the weather was clear and dry. The car seemed to drive itself as my thoughts drifted far away.

After several hours, we reached Colorado. A sign read: Welcome to Colorful Colorado. Jagged cliffs appeared almost instantly, as if magically they knew they must change form now that they were Colorado mountains. Dollops of snow-topped the green and gray peaks.

And then we were off the pass and driving straight through to Denver. I breathed in deeply and exhaled slowly.

I was enjoying the silence of the road. I didn't even want to listen to music. I just soaked in the quiet. The gray asphalt stretching ahead of me was the perfect backdrop for me to continue to reflect on where I'd come and where I was going.

In all my questing, I'd managed to put together some

concepts on every spirituality:

First, it was okay to pick and choose from various spiritual disciplines and adopt the concepts and even rituals that made sense to me. Too often people get dogmatic about their spirituality. Or think they are only able to adopt the spirituality of their childhood. But my personal conclusion was that I could mix and match elements of various spiritual concepts that made sense to me and put them together in a way that worked for me. After all, why not?

I had come to this conclusion naturally as a result of my contact with various healers from different traditions. I would find myself in the grocery store and all of a sudden something Jamie had said at the women's sweat lodge would come to mind. Simply realizing that we were all related would be a clear reminder to be kind to the cashier, the grumpy man ahead of me who took forever to write a check, the frazzled mom with a two-year-old who was throwing a tantrum. I would suddenly remember Jamie chanting *all my relations*. And that would change me.

Or, I would find myself feeling lonely or anxious and I would remember what Martin had told me: that I was on a path and that I should trust it. I didn't have to compare my insides with others' outsides. I could be comfortable and feel good about just being me. My mistakes and missteps were what joined me to the human race and, at the same time, represented lessons that I personally needed to learn from.

Second, I didn't have to call myself anything in particular. I simply believed in a spirit of the universe that was inherently good but at the same time not definable. In general, people like labels and I had once tried to label myself. For example, I was Jewish. But I believed in the healing qualities of nature that the Native Americans championed. I believed in the basic principles of love and tolerance taught by Jesus and the Buddha. I felt that the body contained energy meridians that could be used in healing, as did the ancient Chinese who practiced acupuncture.

At some point, I realized that I didn't need a label for my spirituality and that maybe labels weren't necessary. I could believe what I chose to believe and if it worked for me, that was all I needed.

Third, I could feel it when I was in touch with Spirit. It always hit me like a wave of peace, whether I was at a Pueblo, on the acupuncture table, sitting in a sweat lodge, or on a hike. It always felt the same. It felt like home.

Sometimes I could feel in touch with Spirit in everyday locations and during ordinary interactions. It didn't matter whether I was doing the dishes, in a traffic jam, sitting at my computer at work or on the phone, I found I could and would get hit with a moment of presence without warning that would remind me that I was connected to a universal awareness that was all-encompassing. This would inevitably transport me, if only momentarily, out of the mundane and into the world of the Spirit.

So, my connection to my own spirituality was actually within me. It was portable. I could and would take it with me to Denver. Here I was moving to a new city and creating a new home. Yet, I had a strong sense that I could be home wherever I was because I felt comfortable in my own skin. Being in touch with Spirit meant, in another way of looking at it, that I felt a greater sense of self-acceptance.

In the end, what I'd discovered after living in Santa Fe for seven years was that I was going to live my spirituality. If I wanted to meditate, I would. If I wanted to hike and commune with the trees and animals, I would. If I wanted to soak naked in hot springs or consult with spirit guides, I would.

I had begun to feel connected to an omnipresent consciousness that, while I might not refer to as God, I knew to be Good. And this was enough for me. More than enough.

I saw before me a long, broad highway.

I had come full circle.

ACKNOWLEDGMENTS

I wish to thank Lori DeBoer, for her endless hours coaching me and encouraging me to bring forth my manuscript. I also wish to thank Valerie Rose Johnson for believing in my vision and helping me birth it into the world. This book also could not have come into being without my editor, Alexis Kale, and my website / cover designer, Noah Neumark. Thank you for your support.

I am immensely grateful to my parents, Albert and Bernice Lott, for bringing me into this world and gently guiding me, then letting me go, to find my own True North.

Finally, thank you to my daughter, Ariel Sutherland, for brightening my days. Shine on always!

ABOUT ATMOSPHERE PRESS

Atmosphere Press is an independent, full-service publisher for excellent books in all genres and for all audiences. Learn more about what we do at atmospherepress.com.

We encourage you to check out some of Atmosphere's latest releases, which are available at Amazon.com and via order from your local bookstore:

The Bond: How a Mixed Bag of Foster Kids Became a Family for Life, a memoir by A.M. Grotticelli

License to Learn, nonfiction by Anna Switzer

Between Each Step: A Married Couple's Thru Hike on New Zealand's Te Araroa, a memoir by Patrice La Vigne

Ordinary Zenspiration: Find Your Chill, Find Your Fun, Find Yourself, by April Cacciatori

Waking Up Marriage: Finding Truth In Your Partnership, nonfiction by Bill O'Herron

Eat to Lead, nonfiction by Luci Gabel

A Converted Woman's Voice, nonfiction by Maria Covey Cole

An Ambiguous Grief, a memoir by Dominique Hunter

My Take On All Fifty States: An Unexpected Quest to See 'Em All, nonfiction by Jim Ford

Geometry of Fire, nonfiction by Paul Warmbier

In the Cloakroom of Proper Musings, a lyric narrative by Kristina Moriconi

Chasing the Dragon's Tail, nonfiction by Craig Fullerton

ABOUT THE AUTHOR

S. Mariah Rose has been a professional writer for over thirty years. Rose's work has been featured in *ColoradoBiz Magazine* and the *Santa Fean Magazine*. She has a master's degree in International Communication from the University of Denver and lives in Denver, Colorado.

Rose inspires readers with her compelling book, *Detour: Lose Your Way -- Find Your Path*, a memoir about her journey of spiritual recovery. In it, Rose pursues an increasingly personal spiritual path as she comes to terms with her nonspiritual upbringing. Along the way, she explores universal touch points through various encounters with Santa Fe's eclectic community of gurus and spiritual leaders. "Detour" contains valuable lessons readers can glean from.

Discover how to tap into your own spirituality and explore how a "Detour" can transform your life. www.smariahrose.com

CPSIA information can be obtained
at www.ICGtesting.com
Printed in the USA
LVHW030751260521
688447LV00007BA/357